W9-CCZ-819

DATE DUE

MAR 27 1996			

100M—3-65—58395—Ark.P.&L.Co.

The Poems of William Carlos Williams

A CRITICAL STUDY

THE POEMS OF

William Carlos Williams

A CRITICAL STUDY BY

LINDA WELSHIMER WAGNER

Wesleyan University Press: Middletown, Connecticut

Library of Congress Catalog Card Number: 64–22371
Manufactured in the United States of America
FIRST EDITION

For Paul

Contents

Acknowledgements

My deep thanks must go to William Carlos Williams and Mrs. Williams for their interest in this manuscript, and their co-operation in helping me to complete it.

I wish to thank also Sister M. Bernetta Quinn for reading the *Paterson* chapter and Denise Levertov and Frederick Eckman for their comments throughout. Appreciation is also due Alma Payne, Margaret Petrak, Stanley Coffman, Norman Holmes Pearson, and Richard Carpenter.

Materials from the Lockwood Memorial Library Poetry Collection, State University of New York at Buffalo, and the Yale University Library Collection of American Literature are used by permission of those libraries and Mrs. William Carlos Williams. Miss Anna Russell and Mr. Donald Gallup of the libraries were of particularly valuable assistance. Permission to quote from Dr. Williams' prose and poetry, both published and unpublished, has been given by Mrs. Williams and by James Laughlin of New Directions.

Parts of this book have appeared recently in *Criticism, College English, American Weave, Renascence, Fiddlehead, University Review, South Atlantic Bulletin,* and *The English Record.* I appreciate the co-operation of the editors who have allowed me to reprint them.

LINDA WELSHIMER WAGNER

December, 1963

She loves you
she says. Believe it
—tomorrow

But today
the particulars
of poetry

that difficult art
require
your whole attention.

—WILLIAM CARLOS WILLIAMS

To be of one's own time—nothing seems easier
and nothing is more difficult. One can go straight
through one's age without seeing it, and this is what
has happened to many eminent minds.

—THÉOPHILE GAUTIER

Introduction

WILLIAM CARLOS WILLIAMS is recognized today as having been one of our greatest contemporary poets. His poetry, however, still provides fresh critical challenge because little detailed analysis of it exists. As is often the case with the artist whose work is not easily categorized, there are no terms for many of Williams' practices—a considerable critical handicap. It is ironic that, of the critics who have studied Williams' poetry, many have misinterpreted either the poems or the aims of the poet, and consequently have given the wrong reasons for Williams' greatness. I do not quarrel with the esteem in which the poet is held; I propose only to justify that high opinion by a careful examination of his poetry.

The purpose of this book is two-fold: (1) to show the major reasons for Williams' excellence as a poet; and (2) to disprove the assumption that he was a "typical" poet who wrote "instinctively," with little critical awareness. The second purpose is integral to the first, for Williams was a fine poet at least partially because of his technical facility. He developed his poetic skills through close attention to artistic principles and constant experimentation with them. His prose also reveals his unflagging interest in theory; few authors stated their principles so repeatedly or used them so frequently as Williams. At all times, however, his insistence on a conscious application of theory was tempered with his deep belief in what he termed "an essential part of the poetic process, the imaginative quota, the unbridled, mad— sound basis of all poems."[1] (For Williams' account of the poem's creation, see his essay "How To Write," here reprinted as the Appendix.)

Assuming that a large part of the poetic process is inexplicable and therefore must be attributed to individual genius, I do not intend to negate Williams' natural gifts by emphasizing his theory. But

Williams' theory *needs* emphasizing. Many critics have found his poetry objectionable solely on the grounds that he had no theoretic rationale. Others have read no further than his dictum "No ideas but in things," a phrase which antagonizes the person with philosophical interests. In reality, Williams is only insisting on communication through tangible objects which may be more "real" to the reader than abstract words. As he explains, the artist

> does not translate the sensuality of his materials into symbols but deals with them directly. By this he belongs to his world and time, sensually, realistically . . . .
> Being an artist I can produce, if I am able, universals of general applicability. If I succeed in keeping myself objective enough, sensual enough, I can produce the factors, the concretions of materials by which others shall understand and so be led to use—that they may the better see, touch, taste, enjoy—their own world . . . .
> That—all my life I have striven to emphasize it—is what is meant by the universality of the local.[2]

Williams' concept of the local eventually dominates most of his theory, and provides for it a remarkable consistency through half a century of writing. Williams believed that a man's local culture must provide the materials for his art. As an "imitation" or re-creation of this local, art is to be as near it as possible: colloquial speech rhythms are to determine the poetic line; the objects of the local are to serve as subjects for the poem; the changes within the culture are to be reflected in changes within the poem. Because Williams worked continuously from this belief, his poetry changed not in basic intent but in the techniques through which principles were achieved.[3] But because Williams also considered the contemporary poem but one branch of the timeless body of art, many of his technical implementations fall within categories of traditional poetic devices. Some techniques interrelate fragments into organic wholes; others intensify individual details for sharper emphasis and increased speed; while still others contribute to the effect of indirection which permits the poem to exist as an entity rather than as an instrument of the poet.

Because it is the implementation of principle rather than principle itself that causes change within a body of poetry, my primary concern in this study is Williams' use of language, prosody, and structure. This concern is central to any poem, of course, but especially to Williams' work; the interaction between prosody and the word eventually modifies both the structure and the style of his poetry. A concentration on these areas will also show the unjustness of an opinion still widely held: that, although Williams' critical attitudes may have been "fairly consistent," he progressed in the poems themselves by "a series of shocks."[4] A chronological study of his work will show that while the progress of Williams' art may not have been entirely predictable, it was by no means so irregular and violent as this judgment implies.

The chapters to follow attempt to show the chronological progression in Williams' use of the image; of language; and of measure, line, and structure. I have first separated these techniques arbitrarily for ease of definition. In the concluding chapters, however, they are interrelated—as Williams himself conceived them and used them. The study is therefore almost entirely textual in approach, with major emphasis on the poetry and on Williams' own critical comments in his published and unpublished letters, essays, autobiography, and other prose and in the poetry itself, which often is a vehicle for his ideas on literary art.[5] This method allows primary emphasis to fall on the poems themselves, and reasonably so—for in order to understand any art one must first study the art itself and then relate biography, milieu, and external criticism to it.

CHAPTER ONE

"To Repair, To Rescue, To Complete"

1.

RECENTLY called "the giant among American poets" and "the finest of all contemporary American poets," William Carlos Williams has finally come to be recognized. Although his poetic career began formally with the publication of *Poems* in 1909, Williams wrote for twenty years with little critical notice other than that of his friends, Ezra Pound, Marianne Moore, and Robert McAlmon. When formal critics began to mention Williams, they did so casually, as if motivated more by his companions than by his poetry. Some saw him simply as a member of a school; he was an "imagist," a "romantic," a "primitive," an "objectivist." Others were satisfied to credit him with "a good ear" and a modicum of luck. Still others kept silence, indicating perhaps that the congenial doctor-poet (titles so arranged in their evaluation of his abilities) was beneath attention, an embarrassingly eager novice even after years of practice.

The variation in opinion stemmed partly from the fact that Williams' poems did not slide easily into pre-established categories: he used poetic techniques in new ways so that few criteria for their evaluation existed. Many critics took refuge from the "difficulty" of Williams' work by commenting on his subject matter—an important consideration but hardly the only one. Others made vague, irrelevant statements that only baffled the reader; e.g., Babette Deutsch's early conclusion that Williams' poems had "the sense of brightness on the air, of cool winds and clear waters,"[1] John Ciardi's statement that Williams "relies on his own ear and pulse beat."[2]

Critics, in short, hedged. Perhaps they felt that inexact comment was justified because of Williams' reputation as an "instinctive" poet.

The much-publicized fact that the busy physician typed fragments of poems between office calls and scribbled others on prescription blanks, helped create the character of the "unconscious" artist. And, because ultimately the poetry-making process is mysterious and Williams most assuredly was a poet, some truth is bound to lie in such designations. Readers and critics cannot, however, absolve themselves of critical responsibility so easily. If terminology is lacking, it must be invented.

Because Williams himself believed firmly that poetry was of lasting value, and that a knowledge of technique was crucial to the art, he rose to the challenge of the often invalid criticism he found by writing his own. He felt that in a stage of flux, of artistic "lawlessness" such as existed during the first half of the twentieth century, one poet's experiments were of countless value to others. Therefore his comments about his poems and those of others were aimed from the first at revealing the nature of the poetic process. In consequence, although Williams was vindicating his own jeopardized reputation, he was also building a body of criticism to guide many poets of the future. That he felt his criticism integral to his poetry is evident in a 1950 letter to Henry Wells:

> I think you fail sufficiently to take into consideration my role as a theorist. I think you need a word on that to pull your remarks together. For I think that only by an understanding of my "theory of the poem" will you be able to reconcile my patent failures with whatever I have done that seems worthwhile.[3]

Critics were scarcely receptive to what they considered "interference" by an "irrational" poet. True, Williams did not proceed entirely by logical statement. At times his enthusiasm led him into disproportionate emphasis; and because his system was always open to change (as the poem must be to re-create life), critics complained further. Yet, ironically, Williams' criticism is still the best guide to his poetic practice. No one else has come so near catching the structured quicksilver of his poetry—*structured* in that Williams was a conscious craftsman, *quicksilver* because the living materials of poetry move and change constantly. Williams' criticism is, moreover, basically consistent because it stems from several constant principles: that of the local and that of the poem as a re-creation of the local, achieved through use of the American idiom.

Williams used "local" to mean the poet's natural environment, his culture—both contemporary and historic. All segments of the artist's local were important to him—particularly the men who inhabited it. As Williams often affirmed, "That which is living is that which concerns me. I want to place a value on everything I touch and I want to place the human elements first."[4] T. S. Eliot's comment that "Place is only place" triggered this rebuff from him:

> Place is the only reality, the true core of the universal . . . .
> We live only in one place at one time, but far from being bound by it, only through it do we realize our freedom . . . we do not have to abandon our familiar and known to achieve distinction . . . rather in that place, if we only make ourselves sufficiently aware of it, do we join with others in other places.[5]

Knowledge of and roots in a culture give man a deeper identity, a deeper understanding—"the basis of religion,"[6] in fact. In 1925 Williams published *In the American Grain,* a collection of essays united by the theme of men so rooted in their cultures contrasted with others who were not. For example, the Aztecs were great because of their "earthward thrust," their "primal and continuous identity with the ground itself."[7] The tragedy of the conquering Spaniards was their failure to recognize this greatness; the tragedy of Americans is their failure to realize their origin in America.[8] Because this lack of awareness coupled with an ignorance of their current surroundings leaves Americans inarticulate and crippled, Williams advised, "Let's at least probe our immediate hells to the bottom."[9]

Williams' emphasis on America, however, does not mean that his concept of the local was a nationalistic one. As he wrote in 1939, "America to me means any place, anywhere and just HAPPENS to mean America to me for the simple reason that it is . . . America."[10]

So far as creating the poem is concerned, knowing his culture is but the poet's first step. Then his duty is

> to lift, by use of his imagination and the language he hears, the material conditions and appearances of his environment to the sphere of the intelligence where they will have new currency . . . .
> The commonplace, the tawdry, the sordid all have their poetic uses if the imagination lighten them.[11]

And the primary means of lifting the actual to the imagination is language, the immediate expression of the poet's local. In Williams' case, the American idiom as distinct from English speech was the means of both understanding his culture (through listening) and re-creating it in the poem. As he explained in 1944, "each speech having its own character the poetry it engenders will be peculiar to that speech also."

> When a man makes a poem, makes it, mind you, he takes words as he finds them interrelated about him and composes them—with-out distortion which would mar their exact significances—into an intense expression of his perceptions and ardors that they may con-stitute a revelation in the speech that he uses.[12]

Perhaps more than any other contemporary poet who professed the use of natural speech, Williams worked continuously to capture undistorted language, to avoid speech patterns made "poetic" in any way. This practice grew from his firm belief that "Poetry should be brought into the world where we live and not be so recondite, so re-moved from the people . . . . I want to use the words we speak and to describe the things we see, as far as it can be done. . . . This seemed to me to be what a poem was for, to speak to us in a language we can understand."[13]

In his search for a common language, the American poet can follow no past forms; he must attack precedent, hoping that from the resultant chaos will come "the new seed, the one little seed that counts in the end."[14] Man needs a mode relevant to twentieth-century culture, Williams believed, because he cannot realize his feelings through decadent art. Also, because any locale changes constantly, the poem must be flexible enough to reflect those changes. There can be no precedent for a contemporary mode because the age it represents is itself unique.

Yet, crucial to his poetics is Williams' belief that the necessary destruction leading to the new is *not* the destruction of traditional principles but an extension of them into the present: "It may be said that I wish to destroy the past. It is precisely a service to tradition, honoring it and serving it that is envisioned and intended by my attack, and not disfigurement—confirming and enlarging its application."[15] The resolution of this seeming paradox is possible because Williams visualized a "main body of art to which we must return again and again." His account of St. Francis' successful ministry illustrates his concept of art as a "common stem":

Descending each his own branch man and man reach finally a common trunk of understanding.

The only possible way that St. Francis could be on equal footing with the animals was through the word of God which he preached with fervent breath of understanding. Here was a common stem where all were one . . . . Nor do I think it is especially recorded that St. Francis tried to make the sparrows Christians. When the service was over each beast returned to his former habits.[16]

According to Williams, *methods* of implementing principles can vary, but the principles remain constant. "In a word I believe that all the old academic *values* hold today as always. Basically I am a most conventional person. But the TERMS in which we must parallel the past are entirely new and peculiar to ourselves."[17] The poet's function (to lead the race "by a magnificent organization of those materials his age has placed before him") depends on techniques which grow from his gathering "all the threads together that have been spun for many centuries."[18] And Williams' admiration for Sappho, Theocritus, Aristotle, and other Greek artists suggests that it is classic traditions which form the basis of his own poetic theory.

With true classic emphasis, Williams insisted that the poet must know the techniques of his art and must employ them skillfully. Yet craft alone can never guarantee the successful poem. The best artist, Williams felt, must have two primary attributes: "profound insight into the lives of the people" and "the widest imaginative skill in its technical interpretation."[19] Despite his emphasis on technique, Williams' qualification is significant: the employment of skill too must be a creative process, rather than one of imitation or repetition.

However, because Williams realized that many would-be poets denied the necessity of craft, he emphasized it vehemently. Most of his letters, essays, and lectures warn of its importance:

A poem which does not arouse respect for the technical requirements of its own mechanics . . . will be as empty as a man made of wax or straw . . . technique means everything . . . . The importance lies in what the poem is. Its existence as a poem is of first importance, a technical matter.[20]

Following logically from this belief is Williams' admiration of those writers who considered craft to be essential to poetry: Marianne Moore, James Joyce, e. e. cummings, and—early in his career— Carl Sandburg. For Williams, however, Sandburg was to fall into the same category as Whitman. Remarkable artists in that they broke away from decadent forms, they nevertheless failed to perfect new techniques: they could not construct.[21] Similar failure characterizes the work of Ezra Pound, whom Williams described in 1947 as "defeated in his primary effort." Although he admired many of Pound's poems, Williams believed that his friend's work could be improved through concentration on technique:

> Pound's modus, his technical resources have not increased or developed (or have they?) since his beginnings: he has not evolved any clear poetic method so that his present can stand on his beginnings technically . . . . his present line is repetitious, tiresomely the same or positively decayed: all he has done is to put other, not even new material into his copied forms.

Williams concluded that Pound has failed at times because he neglects "the *means,* upon which my greatest hopes are based."[22]

Of his own poetry, Williams was no less demanding. His constant experimentation proves that he was searching intently, in his rapidly changing age, for the best "means" to the poem. Although a casual reader might feel that some collections of Williams' poems show unreasonably varied styles, most of his technical changes follow one of three generally constant tendencies—*interrelation, concentration,* and *indirection.*

Through *interrelation* Williams unites the many components of his local. He creates a single organism rather than a series of feet or lines or images. One line leads directly into the next, as does one stanza into another; speech measures flow throughout the poem rather than being arbitrarily divided; punctuation serves to define both rhythmic and grammatical units; motifs and symbols relate groups of poems so that the poet's total work is united.

As more and more material is interrelated, quantity must necessarily be limited. The poet must work toward "sharpening . . . his art, removing the inessential,"[23] for in poetry nothing can be redundant. "Prose may carry a load of ill-defined matters like a ship. But poetry is the machine which drives it, pruned to a perfect economy."[24] In *concentration,* suggestion replaces statement; complete sentences may be reduced to fragments, the adjective series to a single word, similes to compounds ("ant-like"). Concentration may also, of course, mean expansion—if the total effect of the poem is intensified through elaboration of one of its parts.

Another characteristic of all art is its compactness. It is not, at its best, the mirror—which is far too ready a symbol. It is the life —but transmuted to another tighter form.

The compactness implies restriction but does not mean loss of parts; it means compact, restricted to essentials. Neither does it mean the extraction of a philosophic essence. The essence remains in the parts proper to life, in all their sensual reality.[25]

Concentration as a principle stems from Williams' belief in the importance of the particular: just as the local is a means to the universal, so the properly-chosen detail can be the means to the whole.

As well as being desirable in itself, concentration is also conducive to a third important effect, that of *indirection*. In 1913 Williams wrote to Harriet Monroe:

Isn't the art of writing titles, as all art is, a matter of concrete indirections made as they are in order to leave the way clear for a distinct imaginative picture? To directly denote the content of a piece is, to my mind, to put an obstacle of words in the way of the picture.[26]

In his criticism, Williams continued to emphasize suggestion and "subtlety," stating that "To add some tag is absolutely repulsive to me."[27] He also believed firmly that a poet's personality should never draw the reader's attention from the poem. To avoid making himself more important than his art, Williams advised a fellow poet:

Do not become involved, too intimately involved, in your subject but hold it away from you as an artist should always do. An artist should always speak in symbols even when he speaks most passionately; otherwise his vision becomes blurred.[28]

As he had written in 1934, "All I'm interested in—or almost all—is impersonally, as impersonally as possible, to get the meaning over and see it flourish."[29]

2.

BECAUSE the principles of Williams' poetics are neither strikingly new nor anachronistic, one may wonder why critics were alternately bemused and angered by them. However, judging Williams' poetry today is very different from judging it midway through his career. A small segment of his work gives one impression; the entire collection arranged chronologically, another. Williams wrote excellent poems throughout the century. He also wrote—and published—less success-ful work, work which he valued for one minor effect rather than for a total impression. A critic reading a single collection might have reasonably been puzzled by its unevenness. For one thing, although Williams worked at all times from his theory of the poem as an organism of interacting parts, his technical emphasis was to shift throughout his career. As he stressed diction, one style dominated the poems; as motion became the core of his theory, a modified style was in evidence.

Williams' earliest poetry gives little indication of what most of his later work was to be like. The first poems are largely derivative, with any innovation occurring in line and measure rather than in diction or subject. His 1909 poems are for the most part built on Georgian traditions, as was his early Keatsian epic which was de-stroyed.[30] The poems describe the abstractions of innocence, simplicity, happiness, and love; the collection is dotted with poems of months and seasons and dedications to mysterious ladies. Williams uses apostrophe, personification, inversion, and romantic diction regularly: "flowery May," "eyelids greet," "rich array/ Like merchant silks."[31] Rhyme schemes and metric patterns are, for the most part, regular.

Some of the poems of *The Tempers* (1913) continue to be mélanges of repetitive devices and techniques; in others, however, Williams used innovations leading to the colloquial speech line. This collection is representative of much poetry written around 1912— reacting against restrictive traditions, poets were giving imagination full play, almost despairingly. Indicative of this unrest and its result-ing demand for innovation was the spontaneous rise of Imagism, a general theory of poetry that directed many poets but curbed none into a formal school. Ezra Pound's "A Few Don'ts by an Imagiste," which appeared in *Poetry* in 1913, established the group with these precepts:

1. Direct treatment of the "thing," whether subjective or objec-tive.
2. To use absolutely no word that does not contribute to the pre-sentation.
3. As regarding rhythm: to compose in the sequence of the met-rical phrase, not in the sequence of the metronome.

The "thing" referred to in the first principle was nominally the object, scene, or person acting as subject of the poem; it was actually the image, "an intellectual and emotional complex" presented "instantaneously."[32] Although many poets associated a static pictorial representation with Imagism, Pound's concept was that of a dynamic image, complete with the associations and tensions of life.

The excitement that the Imagist manifesto created publicly centered on the "free verse" principle, or what was interpreted as such, even though most later comments emphasize word selection. Changes in diction, however, were initially much less evident than those in line and stanza, rhythm and rhyme. Even Williams, though his poetic theory stressed the word, was prouder of his escape from standard rhyme and capital letters than that from poetic diction. Poets were soon to realize, however, that *vers libre* was a misnomer—the poem needed a new structure, a new measure to supplant more conventional arrangements and measures.

While showing at all times his inventive restlessness, Williams' experimentation from 1912 through the next twenty years also shows his identification with the general Imagist principles: he concentrated on diction, using figurative language sparingly in his attempts to capture colloquial speech rhythms. He allowed stanzas to remain regular (quatrains and tercets); his lines were thought units of relatively even length. The word was his primary concern because he believed that language, when transcribed as spoken, is "the origin of form, the origin of measure."[33] The poet has only to "let the words be free . . . . They are words. They will have their way."[34]

Williams' 1922 criteria for judging the quality of the artist illustrate his reliance on diction rather than prosody. The poet must be a man who (1) has "contact," recognizes that "all things go back to the ground"; (2) has "a taste for words and ideas"; (3) is "supported by the basic pyramid of tradition"; (4) does not consider "the intelligence to be a disease"; (5) is not cut off from his source of experience, as were Pound and Eliot; (6) pays "naked attention first to the thing itself"; (7) consciously uses "the detail of . . . local contacts." These principles emphasize the importance of the local, the thing, detail, and the word—with no mention whatever of measure, form, or structure.[35]

Much interested in style at this time, Williams described the dangers of metaphor and simile used indiscriminately, of inversion and allusion, and of figurative language forced into the natural speech line.

His conclusion in 1923 was that the natural in poetry is the ideal—"experiences set down with no more art than that necessary to make the whole a sound functioning body."[36]

Williams found, however, that the natural in diction was often difficult to achieve—primarily because connotative meanings make a reader's response unpredictable. Dismayed by inaccurate interpretations of his poems, Williams attempted to use words so that only one impression was possible. He experimented with surrealistic arrangements which divorced meaning from context and with stark presentations which forced readers to accept the word at its simplest. *Spring and All*, 1923, is one of the most uneven of Williams' books, representing as it does this period of transition. Soon, however, because the bizarre images of his surrealistic poems caused much confusion, Williams turned increasingly to the poem depicting a single thing.

The poem of the limited object which had a predictable effect satisfied Williams for more than a decade. Most of his poems during the late twenties and the thirties were concerned with things presented literally, and they consequently were termed "Objectivist"—a designation relating to both subject matter and point of view. Because Williams dealt primarily with objects in this mode, he became more interested in the structure of the poem: just as the essence of the subject often lay in its "shape," so did the essence of the poem re-creating it.

Williams' interest in structure fortunately outlasted his Objectivist period. During the late 1930's, the poet reached a plateau of inactivity that lasted until 1943. His letters reflect his dissatisfaction with Objectivism and his personal lack of confidence; his critical comments all relate to the need for change. In 1938 he wrote concerning the realignment of his poetic objectives: "I'm a severer critic than I was and I've done the easy part of the work. The rest will be hard as hell. Maybe you'll notice the difference if I ever get to it . . ."[37]

By 1941 Williams had decided that specific structural techniques were essential and that an emphasis on structure, along with an inclusion of the subjective which he had avoided during Objectivism, might provide for him "the difference." In his Harvard lecture he explained: (1) There are many ways of viewing a poem, "all of them misleading unless founded upon structure"; (2) the poem is still "a use of words," but "poetic form . . . [comprises] every use of the word beyond and including its literal prose style. It relies upon structure";

and (3) structural approaches may be divided into the "weak" and the "strong," both phases of a workable method. In the former the poet would use old forms when they were suitable; in the latter he would create new structures, based on the rationale of traditional practices.[38]

Characteristically, Williams put his tentative theories into practice in the poems of the 1940's, *The Wedge* and the early books of *Paterson*. His concern with shape led him into experiments with spatial typography and organization, as well as with both old and new structural arrangements. After much invention Williams realized what kinds of lines and structures were possible and which of them were most suitable for his poetic purposes.

By 1948 Williams took a firm stand on his prosodic theories. He stated then that the "permanent and sacrosanct" area in verse, "the place where the time-lag is still adamant," was structure:[39]

> I propose sweeping changes from top to bottom of the poetic structure . . . . I say we are *through* with the iambic pentameter as presently conceived, at least for dramatic verse; through with the measured quatrain, the staid concatenations of sounds in the usual stanza, the sonnet. More has been done than you think about this though not yet been specifically named for what it is . . . . a revolution in the conception of the poetic foot.[40]

Williams continued that "prosodic values should rightly be seen as only relatively true" and concluded that "perhaps our concept of musical time" is the "only constant" in the theory of prosody.[41]

From this point it is only a step to composition-by-field, the concept which sees the poem as a field with objects arranged so that motion-tension occurs—the objects being the parts of the poem in interaction. Breathing rather than listening, the voice rather than the ear, is the criterion for the line. The syllable is used to determine measure; musical terms replace the designations of poetry. Order which gives shape and yet allows invention is most desired. Charles Olson named this concept "projective verse" and elaborated upon it in 1950.[42]

In 1954 with the publication of *The Desert Music* appeared Williams' "variable foot" used in the triadic line of *versos sueltos*, loose verses. As its name indicates, this measure provides a regular form while allowing flexibility so that speech flow can move unhampered. Actually the pause designations in this line arrangement are only more didactic reminders of the phrasing evident in Williams' best poems of the 1940's. This triadic arrangement seems to answer Williams' concern with control, a problem he had been interested in since 1916 when he refuted *vers libre*. In 1932 he had foreshadowed the triadic line with this description of ideal poetic form: "It must be large enough, free enough, elastic enough, new enough yet firm enough to hold the new well, without spilling."[43]

There are other changes between Williams' poems of the thirties and those of the fifties, one of the most significant being the poet's approach to subject matter. Concentrating on "the thing" and excluding any subjective reaction, Williams had reached a stalemate of pictorial perfection at the close of his concern with Objectivism. He realized then that, although Objectivist technique had forced him to learn accuracy and succinctness, it had also limited his choice of subjects. It had prevented his dealing with what Philip Wheelwright calls "the essentially unchangeable conditions of human insight and human blessedness."[44] In the forties, Williams redefined the poet's relation to the poem and to life. He concluded that nothing was outside the province of the poet, and he proceeded to master the technique of making subjective comment without didacticism, as the poems of his last decade show so vividly.

It may seem strange that a poet termed "difficult," credited with using "inexplicable" techniques, has in reality used only those devices basic to centuries of poetry; yet such is the case. Any survey of Williams' poems shows these technical emphases: his early use of traditional devices like the refrain; his experimentation with point of view, subject, structure, and line; his concern with the total poem; and—always—his demand for the natural idiom. It need hardly be said that none of these principles belongs uniquely to Williams, or to his age of poetry. In fact, I am reminded of Edith Hamilton's summation of the classic aesthetic:

Clarity and simplicity of statement . . . were the Greek poet's watchwords . . . . That a skylark was like a glow-worm golden in a dell of dew . . . would have been straight nonsense to them. A skylark was just a skylark. Birds were birds and nothing else, but how beautiful a thing was a bird, "that flies over the foam of the wave with careless heart, sea-purple bird of spring"!

The Greeks were realists, but not as we use the word. They saw the beauty of common things and were content with it . . . . The things men live with, noted as men of reason note them, not slurred over or evaded, not idealized away from actuality, and then perceived as beautiful—that is the way Greek poets saw the world.[45]

The experimentation of fifty years of writing gave Williams the technical facility to attain this matchless clarity and simplicity, and enabled him to present vividly any subject he chose during the last decade of his life. Yet without his belief in "the authentic spirit of change,"[46] Williams too might have halted, complacent, with obsolete techniques. Instead, he scouted for the vanguard. Because he was never afraid to change his mind, Williams' major concepts were so flexible that he had to modify very few of them. His move from verbal emphasis to structural in the 1940's was his only shift in theory, and that in a theory which was only secondary. Williams' chief principle of the local and its language, and the poem as a re-creation of them, has never needed to change. It too is a classic.

CHAPTER TWO

"The Only Truth"

1.

TRADITIONALLY, the image is integral to any poem. In fact, as indicated by the basic scholastic principle "Nothing is in the intellect that is not first in the senses," an image is necessary for any kind of communication.

Williams considered the image of great importance poetically for several reasons. His chief aesthetic principle was that the poem should re-create a locale comprising tangible objects. The poem, then, should also work through the actual—"no ideas but in things"[1]—and the poetic equivalent of "things" is most naturally the image. As Williams stated vehemently, "the abstract as a thing in itself is a man without a body."[2] *Image* to Williams was, however, never a static concept. He realized that pictorial representations were invalid if they did not partially capture the emotion and movement surrounding objects in life. The accurate artist re-created the play of ideas about the image, thus giving energy to his verbal presentation.

The image was also significant to Williams because of his long interest in graphic art, fostered partly by his mother's love of painting. He belonged to several groups of artists, many of whom—Charles Sheeler, Charles DeMuth, and Marsden Hartley—were close personal friends. His comments about Sheeler's paintings indicate again that he considered painting more than a visual impression: "Any picture worth hanging, is of this world . . . into which we can walk upon real grass . . . . It is in things that for the artist the power lies, not beyond them."[3] Williams later explained, in his poem "Raindrops on a Briar," that, although he was much influenced by his mother's still lifes, he never considered painting to be merely graphic:

> I, a writer, at one time hipped on
> painting, did not consider
> the effects, painting,
> for that reason, static, on
>
> the contrary the stillness of
> the objects—the flowers, the gloves—
> freed them precisely by that
> from a necessity merely to move . . .
>
> a more pregnant motion . . . .[4]

In the correspondences which Williams was to find between painting and poetry, evident in his critical comment as well as in both the technique and the subject matter of his late poems, one of the most striking is this concept of the two arts as active expressions.

For these personal and aesthetic reasons, images are of great significance in any study of Dr. Williams' poetry. A categoric survey of imagery throughout his poems proves how closely he followed his belief that local culture should provide all materials for the poem. His images fall into four groups—nature, man, urban society, and art— all natural divisions of the local. The divisions in themselves are not unusual; what *is* revealing is the poet's shift in emphasis from one subject to another, as well as his presentation of each.

Although Williams early expressed the desire to make "a big, serious portrait" of his time,[5] very early poems show his preoccupation with nature as both subject and source of imagery. His depiction of it as "refuge" indicates his feeling that society was something to evade. Almost from the beginning of his career, however, Williams combined images of nature with images from one of the other subject categories, for one corollary of the principle of the local is that it must be seen as a whole. Few objects exist in isolation, especially in an urban environment where nature is always seen in a configuration of the city and its people. Further, Williams combined the familiar images of nature with subjects that were new to him, relying on nature's "least common denominator quality" to convey his meaning.

Most often nature was coupled with man. In fact, most of Williams' poems deal ultimately with the human state—as does most poetry, even if at times indirectly. All art returns to "human need," as Williams declared: "I go back to the people. They are the origin of every bit of life that can possibly inhabit any structure, house, poem, or novel."[6] Similarly, he valued his medical profession for its access to "real human relations."[7]

In Williams' ethic of humanity, woman is almost mystically essential: she provides the energy for man's creativity, initially through sex but ultimately through a purely feminine accord. Unlike him she has "gentleness and tenderness and insight and loyalty."[8] Dr. Williams' depiction of males, on the other hand, varies significantly. Man in isolation—the sensitive, elemental poet figure—is good; hypocritical man who denies his emotions and his humanity is evil. As society becomes more complex and man's inhumanity grows more obvious during depressions and wars, Williams' censure broadens to include the mass of men, all seen as deadened and monstrous.

Williams also felt that any interest of man must be included in a true depiction of the local: social problems, finance, "the whole armamentarium of the industrial age"[9] become subjects for the poem. Thus his characteristic poems contain images from the worlds of nature, human experience, and urban living, unified finally in the figure of Paterson—man-city-river. But although Paterson is a union of elements, the sign of the times is "divorce," fragmentation, in the disoriented perspectives of most men.

Finally, in the fifties, "to see life steadily and see it whole," Williams like Arnold turned to art; it alone he described as "unchanged and unchangeable . . . . because of the element of timelessness in it."[10] This concern for art* is no contradiction of his emphasis on the local—art of some kind is integral to any culture. And Williams was selective in his admiration of individual artists; his favorites— Cézanne, Dürer, Botticelli, Gaugin, Van Gogh, Brueghel—also worked from their locales and in so doing emphasized human values above all others.

2.

AT the inception of his career, in *The Tempers* as in the 1909 *Poems*, Williams used many nature images taken from tradition—the savage flame, the mystic water figure, the fruit tree representing wealth. He soon left the traditional signification of these objects, however, and

---

* Williams uses the term to mean all forms of art, although he often employs painters to represent the larger concept because of his growing personal interest in graphic art.

applied them to his own culture: the tree which had been the companion to the muse now comforts lonely men. Somewhat later, intensifying the sense of the similarity between good men and nature, Williams changed trees into beasts of love, souls, and people, all identities happy and peaceful.*

Subsequently, association with the tree suggests the attainment of happiness through natural wisdom. Williams employs the image "faces like/ old Florentine oaks" to elevate Negro women, close to life, above the town's leading citizens, whom he describes as "nonentities" with "set pieces" for faces. "Pastoral" repeats the comparison as Williams moves more explicitly into the human world through reference to nature. Here "ingenuous" sparrows are superior to men because they reveal their emotions; similarly, man close to nature ("gathering dog-lime") is superior to man living amid the abstractions of civilization (the Episcopal minister). Innate majesty and dignity are one with the natural in the poet's sight.

Williams had already established the dichotomy which was to serve throughout his life—that between the man who acts with genuine feeling and the one who denies emotion. The few favorable portraits of these early years are of simple people who live naturally: "Canthara," "Portrait of a Woman in Bed," "To Mark Anthony in Heaven." In the last poem, Williams presents Mark Anthony as a normal human being—one whose actions are motivated by emotion rather than logic and are therefore excusable:

> This quiet morning light
> reflected, how many times
> from grass and trees and clouds
> enters my north room
> touching the walls with
> grass and clouds and trees.
> Anthony,
> trees and grass and clouds.

---

* Sister M. Bernetta Quinn sees this metamorphosis of inanimate objects into animate as the revelation of the poet's empathy. The "tendency to humanize nature" is a universal one; "men, and most of all poets, are not satisfied to leave their non-human settings untouched by the imagination."[11] Just as Williams created in Paterson the protean symbol of man-city-river-art and in "The Wanderer" became himself the river, trees find new identities in these early poems.

Why did you follow
that beloved body
with your ships at Actium?
I hope it was because
you knew her inch by inch
from slanting feet upward
to the roots of her hair
and down again and that
you saw her
above the battle's fury—
clouds and trees and grass—

For then you are
listening in heaven.[12]

The pervading gentleness of this poem, in strange contrast to the vehemence usually associated with Mark Anthony, is achieved through the intimate conversational tone and casual direct address and through the poet's evident understanding and acceptance of Anthony's act as merely human. The setting of the poem in the poet's room rather than on exotic Egyptian sands also increases the effect of naturalness, as does the nature imagery used as refrain. In addition to making the refrain a basis for structure and rhythm in the poem, Williams re-arranges the nouns in each repetition to emphasize the surrounding lines, even to the association of Anthony with trees in lines six, seven, and eight.

Nature and its dignity is linked with love and its emotion in Williams' present ethic. Although he does not here stress his belief that the man who denies his humanity is evil, the implication is obvious. Williams reveres honesty and sympathy. And his images show that if man is natural and loving, he will have the motion and warmth inherent to life. These qualities appear throughout the poems, as Williams attributes movement to inanimate objects which he considers "worthy" and withholds motion from undeserving people. The tree, of course, is always animate.

A typical example of the incorporation of these images into one poem is "Danse Russe," in which Williams used the images of flame as creative force (warmth) emanating from nature

the sun is a flame-white disc
in silken mists
above shining trees

coupled with that of the isolated poet, "the happy genius" who dances joyously, all senses bared in nakedness:

> . . . I in my north room
> dance naked, grotesquely
> before my mirror
> waving my shirt round my head
> and singing softly to myself:
> "I am lonely, lonely.
> I was born to be lonely,
> I am best so!" . . .
>
> (*CEP*, p. 148).

From 1910 to 1920 Williams concentrated on self portraits like the above and on descriptions of people whom he admired. During the twenties, however, he turned his attention increasingly to people who had disappointed him and, in contrast, to objects which were powerless to do harm. He wrote then that most men are "fools and their breed is unnumbered. Yet you love them. You can afford to love them because you can understand what they are." Understanding leaves its mark on the poet, however, for Dr. Williams continued: "Disgust is my most moving emotion . . . . I am always, unhappily, knee deep in blue mud."[13] One of the major causes of his discouragement was, quite naturally, World War One. As he wrote, the war not only blots out "everything lovely" but it also exposes "the stupidity, the calculated viciousness of a money-grubbing society."[14]

The poems of the 1921 *Sour Grapes* reflect this simultaneous disgust and compassion. In *I Wanted to Write a Poem* Williams explained his emphasis on man in these poems: "I was very late, very slow, to find out about the world. This book is all about that sort of thing" (p. 33). Marriage and family as well as medical practice had brought him into greater contact with men. It is interesting that Williams again turned to nature for comfort during these years: "there is not much/ that I desire/ the trees . . ./ an expanse of dried leaves perhaps." Of stars he wrote, "I walk by their sparkle/ relieved and comforted."

His depiction of man, generally unfavorable, is conveyed chiefly through images which contrast man and nature, always to man's detriment. During the late twenties, Williams' censure of man extends even to himself:

O river of my heart polluted
and defamed I have compared you
to that other lying in
the red November grass

beginning to be cleaned now
from factory pollution . . . .

That river will be clean
before ever you will be
("11/8," *The Descent of Winter, CEP,* pp. 308-309).

Images showing the crassness of humanity increased during the thirties, becoming progressively more vituperative. Williams wrote of "beastly" men with "black hearts" who, alienated from nature, contaminate and destroy both it and the few people still identified with it. In "Horned Purple," "dirty satyrs" steal lilacs, "breaking the bushes apart with a curse for the owner"; in "At the Ball Game" humanity is pictured as "venomous/ it smiles grimly/ its words cut." "Love has not even visited this country," Williams concludes.

Men who are presented as individuals are viewed externally so that the poet does not see their "black hearts": "I saw/ an elderly man who/ smiled and looked away/ to the north past a house—" Williams chose a seemingly happy man here, but his more usual reaction to humanity permeates "10/29," in which he comments, "The justice of poverty/ its shame its dirt/ are one with the meanness of love."

"Impromptu: the Suckers" shows the compass of Williams' disgust; the poet used a contemporary incident, the Sacco-Vanzetti affair, as a hinge for broad social criticism. "The suckers" are not Sacco and Vanzetti, however, but all Americans who find "solace" in "vile whisky" and "silken crotches"—who do not know their own capabilities, and most assuredly do not fulfill them.

It's no use, you are Americans, just the dregs.
It's all you deserve. You've got the cash,
what the hell do you care? You've got
nothing to lose . . .
(*CEP,* p. 316).

During the thirties, Williams considered man without pride, judgment, or values; therefore the conviction of Sacco and Vanzetti was to be expected. (This was Williams' customary use of specific situations—as examples rather than as content entire; his concern was nearly always with the general human condition.)

The poems of the mid-thirties mark the depth of Williams' disillusion: life is filled with "gross odors," man's mind resembling "a corked bottle." Men continue withdrawing into indifference, causing sensitive people, like D. H. Lawrence in Williams' elegy, to die of life's coldness. Viewing man in the midst of the Depression, Williams saw him as hopelessly depraved—either openly brutal or completely indifferent. Brutality is illustrated in the outright injustice given "An Early Martyr," the cruelty of "The Yachts," the hostility of war and its young men who menace the innocent. In everyday existence, indifference is as flagrant: poor children intent on viewing a beautiful lake as they stand amid the squalor of their home are ignored by passing society; a dead baby is surrounded by "curious holiday seekers."

"The Raper from Passenack" clarifies Williams' opinion of the human position: the victim does not fear pregnancy, re-creation, but only infection. "No one who is not diseased could be/ so insanely cruel . . . . it's the foulness of it can't/ be cured. And hatred, hatred of all men/ —and disgust." Passenack, an industrial center, spawns people without ethics or sympathy. Their disease, inhumanity, cannot be "cured"; it instead breeds further distrust and hatred.

Obviously Williams' feeling was more intense in these poems than it had been earlier. The Depression, of course, revealed more and more of man's cruelty, its results especially evident among the poor of Rutherford who were Dr. Williams' patients. His few pleasant poems of this period deal with these poor yet self-reliant people who withstood economic and social hardships—the old woman comforted by the plums, the old couple out walking. In *I Wanted to Write a Poem* Williams described his reaction to the events of the thirties: "I was impressed by the picture of the times, depression years, the plight of the poor. I felt it very vividly. I felt furious at the country for its lack of progressive ideas" (p. 49).

He recalled, too, that so great was the impact of life upon him that he studied it rather than writing during this decade. His collection of short stories depicting these years is fittingly called *The Knife of the Times*.

As Williams' disgust with man grew, it colored his view of all life. Even nature became cold and lifeless. A "half-broken" tree stands "alone on its battered hummock"; the peaceful country is "broken." "Saddened" by man's actions, nature now "in its barrenness" equals "the stupidity of man." But, once Williams decided that the times were "dark" and "desolate," he again separated nature from contact with man, using it instead as contrast: the wood thrush's song creates "Vistas/ of delight waking suddenly/ before a cheated world"; the sordidness of murder contrasts with "snow trees/ flashing/ upon the mind/ from a clean/ world."

Just as he separated nature from man's contamination, so Williams once again distinguished between the types of men—not all are evil. He used the characters of Adam and Eve, admittedly representative of his own father and mother, to illustrate the chasm between emotional warmth and coldness. Eve has deep emotions; her intense will to live causes her to scream and claw at Time for what life remains. Adam, contrastingly, suffers "the death that duty brings/ so daintily, so mincingly,/ with such a noble air." He goes to his death "coldly/ and with patience—"

It is this cold, silent, passionless man who has contaminated the natural world which he can no longer understand. Such a man, allied with the rigidity of modern urban method and mechanization, can only destroy life. He "civilizes" man and "improves" nature, but nature so modified by urbanization provides only "A Bastard Peace":

> —where a heavy
> woven-wire fence
> topped with jagged ends, encloses
> a long cinder-field by the river—
>
> A concrete disposal tank at
> one end, small wooden
> pit-covers scattered about—above
> sewer intakes, most probably— . . .
>
> (*CEP,* p. 414).

The harshness of the heavy fence and the cinder-field coupled with the cold permanence of the concrete sewage system contrasts sharply and unfavorably with the peace of a typical country scene. Urban peacefulness is ironically enforced by the fence, for few people would trespass on a cinder-field or wander through sewer intakes. To this bleak portrayal of urban life, Williams juxtaposed one of his few poems of nature in this decade. A depiction of a bird "perfect/ in mid-air," suitably allied with love, it is titled "The Unknown":

> Beating heart
> feather
> of wing and breast
>
> to this
> bleakness
> antithetical
>
> In love
> dear love, my love
> detail is all

$$(CEP, \text{p. } 423).$$

Life, in the eyes of any person who sees accurately, is hardly such a rigid dichotomy of good and bad. Williams also showed his ability to view individual man at times as a humorous creature, through the tongue-in-cheek detail of

> Doc, I bin lookin' for you
> I owe you two bucks.
>
> How you doin'?
>
> Fine. When I get it
> I'll bring it up to you.

("Detail," *CEP*, p. 427.)

and the mockery of himself and social convention evident in "The Return to Work" and "Graph for Action." Recurring touches of irony also challenge the most formal of Williams' poems. "It Is a Living Coral" has several fine touches—some comically incongruous metaphors, and a burlesque reminiscent of a side-show barker in the midst of stark history: "It climbs/ it runs, it is Geo./ Shoup/ of Idaho it wears/ a beard/ it fetches naked/ Indian/ women from a river . . . ." The ending of "The Winds" and the modulation at the conclusion of "This Florida: 1924" also illustrate Williams' command of both timing and irony.

"Hemmed-in Males" in particular carries the flavor of Dr. Williams' humor, which always reflects the pathos of the human situation truly understood. Although it supposedly describes a man begging a drink during prohibition, the poem actually depicts man's suffering in society. Pleading for his masculinity as well as his creativity, the poem's *persona* receives only "empty bottles" from what Williams saw to be the stifling atmosphere of the times.

3.

THE changes in Williams' poetic technique between 1938 and 1943 have often been enumerated—a general move from substantive to kinetic, from a reliance on nouns and adjectives to verbs, from a concern with objects to one with actions and broad scenes. Even more significant, however, is Williams' change in attitude toward both man and art. Following such bitter statements of 1937 and 1938 as that the world is "unfit for literature"[15] and "death is not sad. It's life that's sad,"[16] he began emphasizing the need for love. He gave up his early despair at living so long and stated that there was, after all, a little light among people—that contemporary culture, for all its faults, was not "tight, hopeless, sterile."[17]

Just as his dissatisfaction with Objectivist technique forced Williams to find a new mode of expression, so his despair with man forced him into new attitudes. One recourse was suggested in a 1939 letter in which he followed a comment that life was "sour" with a paragraph of loving praise for his wife.[18] The implication was that life was worth while because of Flossie. In his last poems, Williams pursued this lead: he gradually limited his attention to objects and people whom he loved. And he added to his philosophy of love the necessity of the mind, even deifying it in some later poems: "it is in the mind, not on the moon, we must find our relief . . . . The mind's the thing."[19] Eventually, through this union with the mind, love took on the qualities of a religion. As Williams wrote in 1944, man's "moral code" should be "based on our responsibility to our fellow man . . . on the essential value of the individual."[20]

Williams' second recourse was a turn from human interaction per se to art—and his comments indicate his reverence for it as a refuge more stable than nature. As *Paterson* V was to show, art crystallizes and preserves the best of life; it has the virtue so often missing in human relationships. In 1957 Williams wrote that his faith rested in art; somewhat earlier he had described the place of poems in his life: "They are things I wrote because to maintain myself in a world much of which I didn't love I had to fight to keep myself as I wanted to be."[21]

The most dominant change in tone evolving during this five-year period of personal and artistic metamorphosis is that from vituperation to gentleness. In *The Wedge*, 1944, Williams depicts a delicate flower which "splits the rocks," and birds and flowers more powerful than volcanic upheaval. He also asks rhetorically, "Violence and/ gentleness, which is the core? Is/ gentleness the core?"

Most images of this volume and, subsequently, of *The Clouds* and *The Pink Church* reflect a contemplative mood; there is much less bitterness than in previous collections. Williams focused again on nature rather than man, comparing love to a moth, his lover to a river, old age to winter. "Another Year" reflects the serenity of the poet's mood, expressed through images of solitude, quiet, and virtue:

> In the rose garden in the park
> let us learn how little there is
>   to fear . . .
> alone in that still place.
> The slender quietness of the old
>   bushes
> is of a virtue all its own . . .
>
> (*CLP*, p. 56).

When Williams did turn to man as subject in these short poems, his disillusion is less apparent, his tone almost resigned. The pervasive condition of man has not, however, changed: his loveless "idiot mind" is "scurvy"; his actions are "sad" and "unscrupulous." In such a culture, love exists only as "a flower with roots in a parched ground." In "To Ford Madox Ford in Heaven" Williams again restates his praise for the man of emotion. He pictures Ford as a "heavenly man," "filthy with his flesh and corrupt that/ loves to eat and drink and whore"; and thanks God that Ford "was not delicate." Portraits of censure during this decade expose man's falsity—that of the gentlemanly warmonger, the righteous hypocrite, the pretentious artist. Williams also depicted the type of hypocrisy most damning to him: the mind's assumed elevation over the body, "The poor brain unwilling to own the obtrusive body/ would crawl from it like a crab."

For relief the poet turned to animals; he pictured both the horse and the "lonesome" dog with sympathy as they move "independently," "going into new territory," "generally conscious of the world" but not overawed by it. "Education a Failure" presents the urban world dominated by "minor stupidities." In "The Mirrors," written during World War II, Williams asks desparingly, "Is Germany's bestiality . . . any more than a reflection of the world's evil?" So convinced was he of this all-encompassing human evil that the only refuge left was his "dream," again suitably allied with nature:

> Inspired by my dream I do not call upon
> a party to save me, nor a government
> of whatever sort.
>   Rather I descend into
> my dream as into a quiet lake . . . .

But he must dream alone: "While armies rush to the encounter/ I, alone, dream before the impending/ onslaught" ("Russia," *CLP*, p. 93).

Although Williams often expressed a wish to escape from the world, images of his 1948 collection come increasingly from the urban complex. Perhaps because the writing of *Paterson* was so far in progress, with the identity of man-river-city well established, he was more inclined to bring together all areas of life through imagery, as in these passages from "Aigeltinger":

> Deftness stirs in the cells
> of Aigeltinger's brain which flares
> like ribbons round an electric fan
>
>   . . .   the grass
> the rose-cane leaves and blackberries
> and Jim will read the encyclopedia to his
> new bride—gradually . . . .
>
>   (*CLP*, p. 65.)

Urban images infiltrate poems of all subjects, even of nature: "The Willow supplants its own/ struggling rafters"; the poet speaks of the "bare structures/ of a face" and air like "lead." In subject, too, these 1948 poems reflect Williams' new interest—the nude decorating a machine shop, a telephone, stone steps, a bank, a motor barge.

The images of the poems of the 1940's correlate with those of *Paterson* where the interreliance of man-nature-thing is not only the source of imagery but also the theme. In the epic all areas of life are united by the poet's language, as the image "that rafter of a rock's lip" illustrates. Man, however, has no such "redeeming" language. He therefore lives in a fragmented world, disoriented and inarticulate.

The poet searches for a means to aid mankind in communication. He finds no solution in formal knowledge: universities are fallen buds, "suppressed"; the convent has only a "mathematic calm"; the "wadded" library "sweats of staleness and of rot/ a back-house stench." Knowledge-language must reflect life, Paterson knows; it cannot be codified. The poet then looks to the people of Paterson, but they are for the most part lifeless "automatons, Who because they/ neither know their sources nor the sills of their/ disappointments walk outside their bodies . . ./ locked and forgot in their desires—unroused." Men are too apathetic to create anything: love is "a nail in the skull" which only destroys—"flowers uprooted . . . trees dismembered." Interested only in money, man represses and destroys the natural; "flagrantly bored" by life, he is excited only by "the next sandwich."

Ironically, the products of this great industrialization are "shoddy," despite the appalling sacrifice of both nature and man. Williams presented the locomotive, for example, as having an "absurd dignity" in contrast to the "true dignity" of mud. The bleakness of Williams' depiction of man in a mechanized society, building through the poems of the thirties, had been further intensified by the brutality of another war.

Not all men, however, are dulled creatures. The poet finds a "Beautiful thing" in the passionate "drunk and bedraggled" gang mistress—emotion sharp, nature trusting, beauty primitive. Williams' imagery creates parallels between human passion and the natural violence of tornadoes, fires, and floods. And from this personal emotion and natural force comes the redeeming "new seed."

Williams' optimism seems to diminish in Book III as he realizes that man's perversity blocks natural development. All efforts end in a "leaden flood" of purposeless words and activity. Books IV and V, however, show that some men still, through feeling and honesty, can find the virtue in life. Virtue to the young poet had been embodied in nature; later it was incarnated in the body of the "Beautiful thing"; in Book V it is described as "a complex reward . . . achieved slowly," man's best given in creation, a best won only after a lifetime of endeavor. The harmony existing in all art and life depends on virtue; and, because it has the power to "revive" man, he need never die.

Paterson is consequently Williams' full statement of his attitudes toward man. In it he presented the cyclic resolution of his hatred so evident during the thirties: disgust for the lifeless "automatons"; discovery of the few sensitive, humane men; and finally reaffirmation of elements of virtue—whether found in men or in art.

4.

THE three volumes of poems published after 1950 in addition to *Paterson* V—*The Desert Music, Journey to Love,* and *Pictures from Brueghel*—are also united by the need for love among men and for a common language to express that love.

Man now needs language both for a sense of community and for the alleviation of his own suffering: "and so I am assuaged/ from my pain." Most contemporary men, however, come to their deaths in silence while "the bomb speaks." The society Williams depicted in this last decade is dominated by fear and apathy, with men prostrating themselves before "the bomb." The Negro, once identified in Williams' poems with free strength and nature, chokes in a filthy tight collar on a dark city street as the poet asks "how/ shall we/ escape this modern/ age and learn/ to breathe/ again." Mechanized society, symbolized by "the indifferent chap/ with the machine gun/ . . . spraying the heap," has only silent "heroes."

Perhaps because this was the dominant tone of society as he saw it, Williams turned increasingly to objects and people he could love— his wife and grandchildren, pets, flowers, postcards, fellow writers, art. Consequently, although Williams' world of nature, man, society, and art remained constant for fifty years, these late images are much more limited in scope. To maintain himself in an antagonistic world, Williams finally wrote only of virtue—nature undefiled, man as creator, love as generous, art filled with innovation and life. His comment on René Char offers an explanation for this noticeable concentration on the good; Williams admired Char for his belief in "the power of beauty/ to right all wrongs . . . . With invention and courage/ we shall surpass/ the pitiful dumb beasts."[22] As he continued in "The Gift":

All men by their nature give praise.
          It is all
                    they can do.

     The very devils
               by their flight give praise.
                         What is death,
          beside this?

               Nothing.

                                   (*Pictures*, p. 62.)

Williams' emphasis on virtue resulted from the interrelation of nature, love, and art in his life, an interrelation which broadened his earlier perspective. He came to see life as more than a series of laboratory experiments; he saw it as the embodiment of truths which man and poet can only suggest. Although dismayed by the avarice and hatred surrounding him, Williams could still write:

     There is no power
               so great as love
                         which is a sea,
          which is a garden—

However, because his view of the local had been distilled through years of anguished observation, he had also to add:

     Few men believe that
               nor in the games of children.
                         They believe rather
          in the bomb
                    and shall die by
                         the bomb . . . .
          ("Asphodel, That Greeny Flower," *Pictures*, p. 166.)

A sad resignation tempers Williams' confident assertion: there are many who have not realized the power of love, the comfort of virtue. There are, however, many others who have found, with him, that "Death/ is not the end of it," that "the imagination/ and love . . . maintain/ all of a piece/ their dominance."

Because of this belief, Williams focused his final attention on people he loved, on nature, and on art. There was too little time to concern himself with "the world's niggardliness." Instead, as he affirmed, "I lived/ to breathe above the stench . . . ."

This summary view of the images used throughout his poems indicates that the changes in Williams' feelings for man paralleled the degree of his personal awareness and, to some extent, the conditions of his milieu. When a young man, Williams was more interested in placing himself in society than in judging it. Yet, an implicit criticism appeared in even early poems as he turned to nature and solitude in preference to society. His involvement with mankind grew, as it logically would, with his medical practice and his own marriage and family; he soon found the life existing about him impossible to ignore, and—in the midst of war and depression—equally impossible to approve. The imagery of the poems from approximately 1921 to 1938 shows Williams' general dissatisfaction with his milieu and his censure of it, reflected even in images of nature.

The softer criticism of the short poems of the 1940's is balanced by his presentation of man in *Paterson*, Williams' full statement of both his disillusion and his gradual resolution of frustration. The poet's attitudes as expressed in Books IV and V are those of his last poems—that to maintain the self, the artist must turn to virtue even if such concentration means ignoring much of his culture. As evident in *Pictures from Brueghel*, Williams' ultimate recourse from his despair is a concern with objects and individuals he loved and an avoidance of man *en masse*.

In light of his opinion expressed throughout his poems, Williams' final silence about the men who saddened him is more effective censure than any further comment he could have made.

CHAPTER THREE

"Our Wealth Is Words"

1.

As Chapter Two has demonstrated, the sources of imagery in Williams' poetry remained constant, as did the general subject matter evoked by such images: throughout his career, the variable in the construction of his poems was technique.*

Because poetic technique necessarily includes many stylistic and prosodic devices, readers sometimes forget that the successful poet assembles these means under a few guiding principles. For whatever the poet's technical concern at any given moment, the complete poem is his pervasive interest. Williams concentrated on single devices only to achieve total harmony. Such emphasis as his early concern with language, for example, did not negate other technical considerations; he realized the kinetic necessities of the poem but was convinced that words alone controlled movement. Even after 1940, when his theoretic interest appeared to lie in prosody, he still emphasized language: "It is not what you say that matters but the manner in which you say it; there lies the secret of the ages";[1] "style is the substance of writing which gives it its worth as literature."[2]

Of the many issues of style, Williams was most concerned with three: vocabulary, syntax, and figurative language, all of which, he felt, were to be used naturally. And to Williams naturalness was a literal, definable quality. Equating it with the "American idiom," he sought it in the everyday speech of everyday people, and then re-

---

* *Style* as used in this study refers to verbal method—syntax, diction, figurative expression; *meter,* to rhythm of syllable; *prosody,* to that of line, stanza, and structure. *Technique* includes both style and prosody. Unless a contrary definition is given, Williams' use of these terms is similar.

created their speech rhythms and vocabulary in his poems. Colloquial phrasing, figures of speech common to the idiom used, and slang present vividly the subjects Williams took from ordinary existence. Similarly, line arrangement, punctuation, and normal syntax create the fluid rhythms of conversation.

Williams' first efforts toward capturing colloquial speech sounds and rhythms are surprisingly good, especially since his poems of only two or three years before had been larded with archaic "poetic" phrases. In such 1915 poems as "Transitional," "The Revelation," and "Le Medecin Malgre Lui," he achieved idiomatic nuances by using first person narrative focus, simple vocabulary, few adjectives, and punctuation and capitalization dependent on sentence structure. He avoided most figurative language in these poems, probably because of his aversion to any device reminiscent of Georgian artifice. The best of the poems, "Le Medecin," creates a vivid total image through literal expression, a series of verb phrases:

> Oh I suppose I should
> wash the walls of my office
> polish the rust from
> my instruments and keep them
> definitely in order
> build shelves in the laboratory
> empty out the old stains
> clean the bottles
> and refill them, buy
> another lens, put
> my journals on edge instead of
> letting them lie flat
> in heaps—then begin
> ten years back and
> gradually
> read them to date
> cataloguing important
> articles for ready reference.
> I suppose I should
> read the new books.
> If to this I added
> a bill at the tailor's
> and at the cleaner's
> grew a decent beard

> and cultivated a look
> of importance—
> Who can tell? I might be
> a credit to my Lady Happiness
> and never think anything
> but a white thought!

(CEP, p. 36.)

The irony in this poem comes largely from Williams' careful placing of the few necessary adjectives. Of the six, two appear at the poem's center in a phrase stodgily appropriate to the "good" doctor, "cataloguing *important* articles for *ready* reference"; the other four are divided according to the poem's contrast between actual and hypothetical. "*Old* stains" is used early in the poem, opposing the later "*new* books," "*decent* beard," and "*white* thought," the latter joining with the elegant "my Lady Happiness" for the climax of the irony.

The opening line of this complaint, "Oh I suppose I should," is written without the expected comma, which would slow the pace. Williams also omitted commas when they would have fallen at the end of enjambed lines, showing even in these early poems his belief in arrangement as a guide to rhythm and pace. Of course, rhythms are as important as vocabulary in re-creating natural speech, as the various lengths and divisions of sentences here show.

Because of enjambment and omitted punctuation, the impulsive first sentence moves quickly down to the dash: the doctor could do the washing, polishing, building, emptying, and arranging in a relatively short time. But reading through a ten years' accumulation of journals slows the sentence: the isolation of *gradually* coupled with the slower movement of the next lines brings the entire poem to a meditative pace which is intensified by the short sentence. Remaining lines move more noticeably as lines because they are end-stopped. One can almost feel the poet's reluctance to begin each line as his thoughts turn to the trivia which will lead to the final irony.

During the next decade, Williams experimented with natural speech by adapting it to various speakers in diverse emotional situations. One of his most successful poems from this period is "The Widow's Lament in Springtime":

> Sorrow is my own yard
> where the new grass

flames as it has flamed
often before but not
with the cold fire
that closes round me this year.
Thirtyfive years
I lived with my husband.
The plumtree is white today
with masses of flowers.
Masses of flowers
load the cherry branches
and color some bushes
yellow and some red
but the grief in my heart
is stronger than they
for though they were my joy
formerly, today I notice them
and turned away forgetting.
Today my son told me
that in the meadows,
at the edge of the heavy woods
in the distance, he saw
trees of white flowers.
I feel that I would like
to go there
and fall into those flowers
and sink into the marsh near them.

(CEP, p. 223.)

The *persona* in this poem is not the poet but the widow whose soliloquy reflects clearly her state of mind through simple vocabulary and somewhat irrational transitions. The paradox of flaming "cold fire" foreshadows the conflict between bright colors and her life's drabness; the enclosure of the same cold fire foreshadows the conclusion, in which she is smothered both physically and emotionally by whiteness. The widow tries to speak in short restrained sentences but her emotion breaks through three times—once in the initial metaphor, then more forcefully midway through the poem, and finally in the last sentence, where the two *and*'s imply another surge of feeling.

The simplicity of the vocabulary also adds poignancy; it reveals the woman as distraught and inarticulate. One does not question the genuineness of the stark "Thirtyfive years/ I lived with my husband." The contrast of "formerly" and "before" with "this year" and "today," the last used three times in the short poem, stresses the immediacy of the widow's loss.

Structurally the poem is much more complex than "Le Medecin." Williams worked here with two kinds of statement—emotional and descriptive—the juxtaposition of the two serving almost as figurative expression. Beyond the first metaphor, personal narrative precedes factual description, the two sections culminating in the flowers-grief figure. Then the pattern is repeated, leading to the climax in which the sacramental white flowers are correlated with the ultimate of sorrow, the death wish. This use of section as a kind of metaphor, which I have termed "transitional metaphor"* for ease of reference, occurs often in later poems. The alert reader assumes that the poet has a reason for this positioning, and so relates the two sections.

2.

To Williams, all linguistic issues common to poetic criticism were subordinate to his re-creation of the American idiom. It is because of this singlemindedness that both Williams' poems and his vocabulary within them are difficult to categorize.

For example, Josephine Miles' study of the language of poetry in the 1940's provides little information about Williams' verbal techniques: she places him in "the middle group of . . . slight adjectival emphasis"[3] because his part-of-speech ratio is five adjectives to eight

---

*In arranging seemingly unrelated passages so as to suggest a sequential relationship, Williams forces the reader to create his own transition between sections. A typical example is the position of sentences within "Drink":

My whiskey is
a tough way of life:

The wild cherry
continually pressing back
peach orchards.

I am a penniless
rumsoak . . . .

(*CEP*, p. 140.)

Here Dr. Williams relies on the impact of consecutive images rather than any logical progression of "meaning." Like metaphor in that the reader experiences the poem through suggestion rather than didactic statement, this technique of juxtaposition makes comparisons not only without the comparative word but also without the connective.

nouns and four verbs. Although the number of each part of speech is low, the proportion makes of him a "substantive poet," one who concentrates on the static object, with poetic line and movement subordinated to sight impression.[4] Frederick Eckman, however, in his discussion of modernist verse places many of Williams' late poems in the kinetic mode. Characterized by motion, kinetic verse relies upon verbs and verbals in lines determined by the poet's personal sense of movement rather than by any regular meter.[5]

As this disagreement between good critics shows, many of Williams' poems cannot be categorized, except very generally. With Williams, subject matter determined treatment. When he wrote of an active, vigorous person, movement established through verbs dominated the poem:

> The old black-man showed me
> how he had been shocked
> in his youth
> by six women, dancing
> a set-dance, stark naked below
> the skirts raised round
> their breasts:
>   bellies flung forward
> knees flying! . . .
>
>   ("Canthara," *CEP*, p. 143.)

When he wrote of unpleasant people or experiences, he depicted them in stasis:

> This is the time of year
> when boys fifteen and seventeen
> wear two horned lilac blossoms
> in their caps—or over one ear
>
> What is it that does this?
>
> It is a certain sort . . . .
>
> Dirty satyrs, it is
> vulgarity raised to the last power . . . .
>
>   ("Horned Purple," *CEP*, p. 273.)

Williams' ethic of motion as indicative of life, described in Chapter II, partially determines his use of parts of speech. During the nineteen-twenties and thirties, when he viewed mankind with increasing despair, he often presented subjects in death-like poses—hence, "substantive" verse.

Because of Williams' attitude toward subject matter, he probably did rely more heavily on nouns than verbs in the poems of these depression years. But choosing a nominalistic method of presentation by no means implied a dearth of linguistic skill. His very early poems had already proved his mastery of language:

Dawn

Ecstatic bird songs pound
the hollow vastness of the sky
with metallic clinkings—
beating color up into it
at a far edge,—beating it, beating it
with rising, triumphant ardor,—
stirring it into warmth,
quickening in it a spreading change . . .

(*CEP*, p. 138.)

Willow Poem

It is a willow when summer is over,
a willow by the river
from which no leaf has fallen nor
bitten by the sun
turned orange or crimson.
The leaves cling and grow paler,
swing and grow paler . . . .

(*CEP*, p. 196.)

Through expert use of both figurative and literal expression, Williams is able to prevent these descriptive poems from being merely pictorial. He has recognized that verbs rather than nouns create motion. Although these two poems have approximately the same length and the same number of adjectives, "Dawn" pounds along stridently on verbs and verbals while "Willow Poem" moves more quietly on subdued action-words—linking or passive verbs. "Dawn" contains long, sharply accented words filled with plosive consonants, while "Willow Poem" is dominated by the sounds of *w* and *s* as well as vowels. In "Dawn" Williams also uses present-tense verbs with *-ing* endings coupled with dashes to increase the sense of motion. If kinetic description does dominate Williams' late poems, it has its beginning here.

Much the same comparison might be made of poems from later periods, "The Descent" and "The Sparrow," for example. Again and again, Williams' poems prove that his verbal technique varies according to subject and point of view, regardless of chronology.

Rather than emphasizing the use of one part of speech over another, Williams was primarily interested in word choice itself. Many of his short poems are little more than re-creations of speech, words serving as characterization:

> Whyn't you bring me
> a good letter? One with
> lots of money in it . . .
> ("To Greet a Letter-Carrier," *CEP*, p. 432.)

> I had a misfortune in September,
> just at the end of my vacation.
>
> I been keepin' away from that for years . . .
> ("Detail," *CEP*, p. 428.)

> My parents had nine kids
> and we were on the street
> That's why the old bugger—
>
> He was twenty-six
> and I hadn't even had
> my changes yet . . .
> ("Invocation and Conclusion," *CEP*, p. 105.)

Williams used the same techniques when the poem was written in first person, the vocabulary suiting the kind of *persona* he was presenting—from brusqueness:

> If you can bring nothing to this place
> but your carcass, keep out.
> ("Dedication for a Plot of Ground," *CEP*, p. 172.)

to cynical matter-of-factness:

> . . . What in the form of an old whore in
> a cheap Mexican joint in Juarez, her bare
> can waggling crazily can be
> so refreshing to me . . .
> ("The Desert Music," *Pictures*, p. 116.)

and deeply poetic perception:

> this, following the insensate music,
> is based on the dance:
>
> an agony of self-realization
>
> bound into a whole
> by that which surrounds us
> ("The Desert Music," *Pictures,* p. 109.)

Each excerpt is noticeably laconic, regardless of subject. Williams' rationale of conversation—evident in his fiction as well as his poems—is that normal interchange is extremely brief and seldom denotatively meaningful. He censured Hemingway's "unrealistic" reproductions of conversation because "it is rarely as expressive as he makes it and almost twice as succinct."[6]

Williams used colloquial speech expressions when appropriate: "lots of money," "a guy"; "misfortune" and "changes" rather than more exact terms; profanity; poorly enunciated words like "keepin'." He also used slang: "Atta boy!" "Easy girl!/ You'll blow a fuse." His criterion for such expression was that the poet should use as much slang "as suits his fancy or his need, and no more."[7] Williams did not use colorful phrases for local flavor; he used them when they were necessary to characterization.

A "really very simple language,"[8] one avoiding "delicate mincings" and "weighty sounding apostrophes,"[9] was Williams' aim at all times. His translations provide some of the most interesting examples of his concept of the American idiom, as "Theocritus: Idyl I" shows. The excerpts which follow are alternate versions, the first from W. Douglas P. Hill's recent translation, *The Idylls of Theocritus* (Eton, England, 1959), 1-2;[10] the second from Williams' poem, pages 102-107 in *Pictures from Brueghel.*

Hill translation:

Thyrsis: How sweet the whisper of yon spring-fed pine;
      Sweet, too, O goatherd, are thy melodies,
      And only Pan can wrest from thee the prize.
    If his the horned goat, the she-goat thine;
      Choose he the she-goat, thine the kid, whose meat,
      Ere it be milked, is sweet.

Williams translation:

Thyrsis: The whisper of the wind in
                    that pine tree,
                            goatherd,
            is sweet as the murmur of live water;
                    likewise
                            your flute notes. After Pan
            you shall bear away second prize.
                    And if he
                            take the goat
            with the horns,
                    the she-goat
                            is yours: but if
            he choose the she-goat,
                    the kid will fall
                            to your lot.
            And the flesh of the kid
                    is dainty
                            before they begin milking them.

Hill:

Goatherd:

            Nay, shepherd, nay; we may not pipe at noon.
            This is the hour when Pan, the hunter, wearied,
            Rests from the chase; we fear to break his rest,
            So quickly is he vexed, so choleric.

Williams:

Goatherd:

            No, shepherd,
                    nothing doing;
                            it's not for us
            to be heard during the noon hush.
                    We dread Pan,
                            who for a fact
            is stretched out somewhere,
                    dog tired from the chase;
                            his mood is bitter,
            anger ready at his nostrils.

Hill:

            And next engraved an aged fisherman
            Stands on a rugged rock and eagerly
            Draws close his heavy net to make a cast;
            Strongly he toils . . . .

Williams:

there is fashioned there
  an ancient fisherman

and a rock,

  a rugged rock,
   on which

with might and main
  the old man poises a great net
   for the cast

as one who puts his whole heart into it.

One striking difference in the translations is Williams' insistence on normal sentence order in contrast to Hill's inverted structure. Hill also uses archaic pronouns and hyphenated adjectives, whereas Williams turns to contemporary pronouns and prepositional constructions: "sweet the whisper of yon spring-fed pine" becomes "the wind in/ that pine tree,/ goatherd,/ is sweet as the murmur of live water." As this line also shows, Williams characteristically uses more concrete terms: "flute note" instead of "melodies," "stretched out somewhere" instead of "rests." And some of Williams' colloquial flavor comes from his use of slang and figurative speech: "nothing doing" for "nay," "dog tired" for "wearied," "as one who puts his whole heart into it" for "eagerly."

Because Williams felt a definite affinity with the Greek poets, considering their art timeless and consequently contemporary, he expressed Theocritus' words in rhythms as close to his own American idiom as possible. He used the same devices in his translations of Sappho's poems: normal sentence order and vivid concrete expressions achieved through common vocabulary, slang, and figurative speech— in short, through substitution of the idiomatic for any poetic device that seemed unnatural in contemporary conversation.

A second of Miss Miles' conclusions which she applies to Williams' poetry is that the substantive poem is generally free from abstractions.[11] To her statement, one can answer only that Williams' poems often deal with the abstract, though it is frequently exemplified by the concrete: "no ideas but in things." Usually a vivid image represents the term, although the concept itself—old age, love, violence—is named somewhere in the poem. Williams' censure of a young poet's use of the word "beautiful" reveals his dislike of the bald designation used alone:

"Beautiful" is an empty word today. Beauty is something
else again. But we've had enough of "beautiful" for a long
time to come. Your last line, "and is more beautiful," is
weak as hell to my mind. Nothing to it.[12]

Williams' objectification of ideas through imagery saves his poems
from being trite or prosaic. No reader can deny, however, that much
of his work—except for some Objectivist poems—deals with abstractions.

In "Prelude to Winter," for example, he successfully links concretion with abstraction, conveying metaphorically the soft, still delicacy
of love:

> The moth under the eaves
> with wings like
> the bark of a tree, lies
> symmetrically still—
>
> and love is a curious
> soft-winged thing
> unmoving under the eaves
> when the leaves fall.

(*CLP*, p. 55.)

As Williams continued to write about the abstractions of chief
interest to him, the concrete images which he used came to have an
almost symbolic impact. At times the sparrow represented the poet;
again, it conveyed religious significance; in another passage, it stood
for bravery. Although the literal referents are different, they have
qualities in common; they are not contradictory. With the image itself
serving as nexus, each new equivalent adds to the composite definition,
reinforcing the impression derived from previous uses. To avoid confusion with the generally-accepted literary meaning of "symbol," a
word having a consistent though inexplicable referent, I have called
Williams' expanded use of the image "symbolic metaphor."

Flowers, for example, are of central significance through Williams'
half century of poetry. At times they are used metaphorically in that
they are said to be something else: "the yellow flower" provides
escape for the artist, the "familiar flower" warms young lovers, roses
indicate seasons as well as kinds of love, America when newly discovered was a "flower in April," the poet's gift is "a rose/ to the end
of time," and "the image of the rose" is the object of the poet's

"striving." Love is "a weakest flower" as is the poet, at times like the simple asphodel (frail but enduring), at times "a pink locust . . . . a flower/ incredibly resilient/ under attack!" Again, Williams uses the image ambiguously, referring simply to "the flower." The reader must then give the image meaning, based on both its previous associations and its present context.

Like several other contemporary poets, Williams avoided the more traditional literary symbol because he believed such a device excluded the uninitiated reader and made the poem "esoteric." He felt that no figures of speech should be "permitted to intervene between the accepted meaning of the word and the sense in which it is to be understood."[13] For that reason, Williams' symbolic metaphor can be read literally as well as with the periphery of association that knowledge of his total work brings.

3.

BEING governed by his constant rule—that poetic language was to stem from the spoken idiom—Williams easily justified the use of abstractions: people use them, and for good reason: they express large concepts directly and succinctly. As has been pointed out, all Williams' verbal techniques were aimed in part toward achieving economy. Versions of poems from his worksheets show that his revision process is a constant limiting, an endless sharpening. Seldom does a late draft expand upon the original subject matter. Verses two and three of the opening four, for example, are deleted in the final copy of "Eternity":

Early version	Finished poem

She had come, like the river
from up country and had work
   now
in town—
	She had come, like the river
	from up country and had work
	   now
	in town—

implored his aid, frightened at her job, in a rush of work.	When? Tonight. (*CLP*, p. 36.)
He passed her desk thereafter they had talked, he lingered, she clung to him	

When? Tonight.
    (UB Collection
    Roll 21, Microfilm.)

Because the subject of the poem is the poet's emotion in relation to the present happening, the illicit meeting, most background is extraneous. The action itself should reveal both the situation and the protagonist's emotions. As Williams wrote:

> In telling the incidents that occurred to people, the story of the lives of the people naturally unfolds. Without didactically telling what happened, you make things happen on the page, and from that you see what kind of people they were. . . . You can't tell what a particular thing signified, but if you see the thing happening before you, you infer that that is the kind of thing that happens in the area.[14]

Another excerpt from this early draft also shows Williams' initial tendency to slant presentations too obviously, both through word choice and repetition:

Early version	Finished poem
The street was nuts dark, she was late, two young ~~chaps~~ had cavorted	The street was dark, she late. Two young rips
down the hill in the silence laugh- ing jabbering, talking gesticulating, cutting capers grotesquely.	had cavorted down the hill in the silence, jabbering.

One detail of action provides sufficient contrast just as one verb suffices in the early lines. It is typical that the only word Williams replaced in the final poem, *nuts*, had dissatisfied him initially. As he polished, he omitted words rather than replacing them; his revision process shows clearly his search for precise language. As Williams wrote, "The skill of brevity requires deep feeling—or it is jargon. Clearly see (and feel) a hint (pointedly) is enough, more would be too much."[15]

Early versions of poem after poem show the poet excluding entire segments of work in progress. As in the following versions of "Hard Times," most of what Williams came to consider extraneous is either

highly personal material or explicit commentary on something suggested elsewhere in the poem:

Early version	Finished poem

... a fat boy
in an old over-
coat a butt between
his thick lips stands

with hands
in pants pockets
pushing back the
coat kidding

Parking space!
three steps up
from four others
bunched on

the wet pavements
before the
gaping weedy rain
soaked emptiness
        (UB Collection,
           Worksheets.)

...
a fat boy in

an old overcoat, a
butt between
his thick lips, the
coat pushed back,

stands kidding,
Parking Space! three
steps up from his
less lucky fellows.
        (*CLP*, p. 90.)

As in "Eternity," Williams here at first included much unnecessary
detail; in the final version he deleted the cause for the coat's disarray
and the enumeration of boys. The most striking change not only
shortened and sharpened the image but also avoided a maudlin
emphasis on deprivation—"on/ the wet pavements/ before the/ gaping weedy rain/ soaked emptiness" replaced by "less lucky fellows."

4.

CONSISTENT with another of his basic artistic tendencies—that the
poem is to create an immediate relationship with the reader, *without*
interference from the poet—Williams avoided unnecessary commen-

tary, background, and subjective impressions. In 1913 he wrote that art was to be "a matter of concrete indirections." Somewhat paradoxically, the more *direct* a presentation—i.e., immediate, free from didacticism—the more *indirect* it becomes in that no discursive remarks or asides interfere with the reader's response. The poet must interpret the facts, the objects of existence, in order to create meaningful art; yet in so doing, he finds didacticism and sentimentality difficult to avoid. Attaining a balance between necessary objectivity and equally necessary subjectivity was to occupy much of Williams' concentration during his writing career.

Very early poems center on Williams' personal reaction to his subjects; instead of the housewife's existing in relation to the "fish man" or the "walls of her husband's house," she is a "fallen leaf" in the poet's imagination. Often Williams used figures of speech to create a more vivid response. In "The Ogre," for example, the relationship between the poet and the "Sweet child,/ little girl with well-shaped legs" is described as "brushings/ of fine needles."

Somewhat later, however, Williams allowed his characters to speak for themselves, as in "Fish" and "Portrait of a Woman in Bed." He also avoided subjective comparisons and narrated events objectively. This move from the poet-interpreted subject to the factually-presented one was in keeping with his pervasive theory that every word be essential. As a result of this emphasis, many of the poems of the thirties are quite short. Yet, although impersonality may increase the physical reality of the person or object presented, it also may repress or limit the poet's responses and expression. Consequently the results of the poetic process are often still-life descriptions rather than poems. Lines like "Six whittled chickens/ on a wooden bat/ that peck within a/ circle" may create accurate depictions, but they hardly constitute great poetry.

The stalemate into which Williams' concentration on "indirection" led him (at the close of Objectivism) brought about a new evaluation of the poem and of the poet's role in its creation. Williams realized that his opinions and emotions, as integral parts of his local, had legitimate places in the poem. In *The Wedge,* his first collection of poems published after his new definition had been formulated, he struck a balance between involvement (often expressed figuratively) and objectivity, as "A Cold Front" illustrates:

> This woman with a dead face
> has seven foster children
> and a new baby of her own in
> spite of that. She wants pills
>
> for an abortion and says,
> Um hum, in reply to me . . .

The blunt narrative tone helps maintain a semblance of objectivity even while re-creating the mood of tiredness. The phrase "in spite of that" heightens the situation. The poem is not mere visual detail, however; it builds toward a key central simile:

> She looks at me with her mouth
> open and blinks her expressionless
> carved eyes, like a cat
> on a limb too tired to go higher
>
> from its tormentors . . .

(CLP, p. 57.)

Although the rest of the poem returns to literal expression, the simile dominates its effect. Williams' changed concept of involvement is evident in this central figure of the tired, tormented animal, the poet's *interpretation* of objective detail.

Later poems show Williams honing this technique to perfection. In fact, the poet's expressed consciousness became highly significant; it was the power that gave "order" to the "facts" of observation. Dr. Williams' techniques of design as well as his subject matter demanded increased subjectivity. *Montage,* for example, reveals the poet's mind through the choices he must make to determine content and arrangement. While many choices are readily explicable, others appear to have only a tenuous connection with the poem. Consequently, the "associational" value of an object, against which Williams had inveighed in 1920, became one of the bases of his art—this poet who at one time approached even self-portraiture objectively.

Williams as personality also became more important in late poems, a change necessitated in part by his belief that "Age should be a commentator and what better than to comment upon one's own existence."[16] Such lines as "I noticed," "I suspected," "I saw" give the poet a role as participant as well as observer. Many poems record experiences in which personal reactions are the core of the entire poetic experience. In others, Williams appears as both *persona* and speaker:

>a bunch of violets clutched
>in your idle
>hand gives him a place
>
>beside you which he cherishes
>his back turned
>from you casually appearing
>
>not to look he yearns after
>you protectively
>hopelessly wanting nothing

("Suzy," Pictures, p. 21.)

In these late poems, the conflict between indirection and subjective interest was resolved when Williams realized that involvement does not necessitate sentimentality. Language itself can establish the line between naturalness and excessive rhetoric.

5.

ALTHOUGH indirection caused Williams much concern, by far the most troublesome stylistic area in his search for natural expression was figurative speech. His basic decision concerning its employment was simple—that one used it when there was a need for it. Actual practice, however, brought many problems.

Williams first was forced to differentiate among kinds of figures. Surviving what was generally thought to be an Imagist taboo against figurative speech, he followed Pound's command to "Use either no ornament or good ornament." "Good" figures were any which were well used, most often metaphors. Like most poets before and since, Williams preferred metaphor, the relation of dissimilar images, to the "vegetable coincidence" of simile.[17] Like alliteration, hyperbole, and apostrophe, simile was too consciously rhetorical: the best language for the poet, Williams believed, is the conversational. That language, of course, could reasonably include figurative expressions natural to the idiom expressed. Figures of speech also were traditionally necessary for economy or for enriched meaning, as these two versions of "The Manoeuvre" illustrate:

Early version	Finished poem
I saw the two starlings	I saw the two starlings
coming in toward the wires.	coming in toward the wires.
But at the last,	But at the last,
just before alighting, they	just before alighting, they
turned in the air	turned in the air together
and landed, together, back-	and landed backwards!
wards! that's what got	That's what got me—to
me—to face the direction	face into the wind's teeth.
from which they had appeared	(*CLP*, p. 88.)
from which also	
a cold wind was blowing.	
(UB Collection. Roll 21,	
Microfilm.)	

Although Williams distrusted figurative language because it revealed much personal feeling and was often artificial, he eventually
came to accept it as an essential poetic device:

> I speak in figures,
>   well enough, the dresses
> you wear are figures also,
>   we could not meet
>   otherwise. When I speak
> of flowers
>   it is to recall
>   that at one time
> we were young . . .
> ("Asphodel, That Greeny Flower," *Pictures*, p. 159.)

In fact, his employment of figurative speech is so central to his poetry
that a comment like Karl Shapiro's is only puzzling: writing in 1952,
Shapiro stated that Williams shed "figurative language as a snake
sheds its skin; henceforth [from 1930] he is naked, a poet without
decoration, without metaphor."[18]

Shapiro was, of course, exaggerating with reverence as he praised
Dr. Williams for reaching the elusive common idiom. The true situation is, however, that Williams never abandoned figurative language;
instead he used it with increased frequency and skillfulness. Actually,
figurative speech became so important to him that he used it as a
basis for structure (see Chapter IV). Probably because Williams did
consider figurative speech both a structural device and a verbal one,

critics could overlook it in some of his poetry: integral to the poem as a whole, it is relatively inconspicuous. And also, because Williams drew his figures from usual categories of subject matter, they are even further absorbed into the effect of the total poem.

Working from traditional poetic principles, Williams first used figurative speech to broaden content. In very early poems he treated nature metaphorically because he thought of the natural scene as living. Depicting men he disliked often required "reverse personification" so that they would appear inert and lifeless; at the same time, he expressed favorable opinion by giving movement to inanimate things. As well as continuing his ethic of movement to reflect life, Williams also used his categoric approach to subject matter (dividing content into the four separate areas of man, nature, art, and urban society) in constructing metaphors: leaves were "little yellow fish"; the sun was "the bird's companion."

By 1920, however, Williams was using metaphor to interrelate these arbitrarily divided areas so that the actual conditions of life could be more accurately re-created: he spoke of "white thighs of the sky" and considered old age "a flight of small, cheeping birds." Such interrelation reached a culmination in Williams' epic, *Paterson*, where he presented a single character who was man, city, nature (river), and art. And because Williams knew that—although the poem was ostensibly to re-create its surrounding local—any culture comprised more than tangible objects, he dealt here with human values as well as with "things." Consequently, all concerns of life are represented by the single protean metaphor, Paterson.

Williams' means of expressing the objects of broad and often abstract significance with which he was increasingly occupied was a device I have earlier termed "symbolic metaphor," the "polysemous" use of a noun: many meanings which interrelate and support each other (see pages 47 and 48). For example, the "rose" as Williams used it might represent a literal flower, love, personal fulfillment, the poet, religion, the poem, or any combination of these, depending on context. Once the poet established "multiple meanings" for an image, he easily enriched later poems by using that image ambiguously, with no single meaning specified.

"To Be Recited to Flossie on Her Birthday" shows the suggestive quality of the rose image and gives insight into what Williams meant

when he wrote that he desired "to find some basis for avoiding the
tyranny of the symbolic without sacrificing fullness of imagery."[19]

> let me say
> across cross purposes
> that the flower bloomed
>
> struggling to assert itself
> simply under
> the conflicting lights
>
> you will believe me
> a rose
> to the end of time

(Pictures, p. 35.)

The rose, Paterson, the sparrow, the unicorn, and many other images
become more than representationally meaningful in Williams' late
poems. The poet had moved beyond traditional use of figures of
speech. His rationale of metaphor enabled him to fuse tangible with
intangible and to present life as a timeless, indivisible whole.

CHAPTER FOUR

"It Is a Design"

1.

IMPORTANT though metaphor is to the content of Williams' poems, it is even more significant as a principle of organization. All Williams' comments about the figure stress its ability to increase both the depth and the speed of the poem. He saw metaphor as an integral part of the poem's "anatomy," never an "addition" to it. As he wrote in "Preface to a Book of Poems," metaphor identified with "all the pretty glass balls, all the thrilling details of writing verse, must today be subjugated to . . . the structure of ideas."[1]

It is difficult to find a metaphor in Williams' poems which does not have structural importance. Most figures hold prominent positions in the poem, falling at the beginning, center, or end. Often the figure is isolated dramatically in the midst of literal expression, gaining much force from the contrast between kinds of speech.

Dr. Williams did not use metaphor for shock effect, however, as T. E. Hulme had once conceived of its value. Non-figurative lines relate to the metaphoric image, either by anticipating it or by elaborating it, so that the metaphor is the core of the entire poem. Frequently the isolated figure appears at the end, with detail building toward it, as in "A Negro Woman":

> carrying a bunch of marigolds
> wrapped
> in an old newspaper:
> She carries them upright,
> bareheaded, . . .
> as she walks

```
looking into
        the store window which she passes
            on her way.
What is she
    but an ambassador
        from another world
a world of pretty marigolds . . .
```
(Pictures, p. 123.)

Literal lines lead to the concluding metaphor as Williams describes the woman with fitting simplicity and dignity. She carries the flowers proudly, "upright"; while she walks, she looks about her—curious and attentive. The literal description indicates that she is well suited in her dignity to be "an ambassador" and, in her naturalness, to represent "a world of pretty marigolds."

Dr. Williams often used a complex of metaphors in which one was structurally dominant, with the others acting to expand the chief figure. As a rule, the dominant figure of several occurs early in the poem so that its relationship with the others is clear. "The Pink Locust," for example, begins with the simile, "I'm persistent as the pink locust," the comparison between the poet and the flower being the subject of the poem. Other figures—all related to the initial comparison—occur at intervals throughout.

From this basic structure grew several types of organization. The simplest is the elaboration of an initial metaphor, to be found in "To Waken an Old Lady":

```
Old age is
a flight of small
cheeping birds
skimming
bare trees
above a snow glaze.
Gaining and failing
they are buffeted
by a dark wind—
But what?
On harsh weedstalks
the flock has rested,
the snow
is covered with broken
seedhusks
```

and the wind tempered
by a shrill
piping of plenty.

(*CEP*, p. 200.)

The effectiveness of this poem results from the purity of the single metaphor carried throughout, non-figurative lines in keeping with the figurative. Through the careful progression of detail, the last nine lines quietly reverse the direction of the opening, resolving the poem so that it *is* well suited for its purposes. Because of Williams' expert choice of adjectives, the shift after the interrupting question is gradual; *harsh* weedstalks continues the tone of early lines, as does *broken* seedhusks when read in the early context. That the flock has rested and has access to seeds, however, turns the poem toward the concluding "piping of plenty."

Vivid as this depiction is, it presents a relatively simple experience; such structure can be used with only limited subjects. Consequently, Williams expanded his use of metaphor as structure by juxtaposing images which employed singly each of the subjects fused in the metaphor. "A Widow's Lament in Springtime" (see p. 38) utilizes this device, as does "Love Song."

Sweep the house clean,
hang fresh curtains
in the windows
put on a new dress
and come with me!
The elm is scattering
its little loaves
of sweet smells
from a white sky!

Who shall hear of us
in the time to come?
Let him say there was
a burst of fragrance
from black branches.

(*CEP*, p. 137.)

Drawing from the subject areas of human relationships and nature, Williams gives the entire first strophe a domestic orientation. Especially striking details are the cleanliness of the sky and the elm's "loaves/ of sweet smells"—a figure effective for its reversal as well as its coupling with the elm. (The expected order would be "sweet smells of loaves.")

Although no metaphor has specifically united the lovers with nature, the position of the four-line nature description immediately after the poet's invitation suggests the intended relationship. In the second strophe, by "answering" the poet's question with another nature description, Williams again uses juxtaposition, heightened here by a new intensity in the familiar image of smell. Now that the lovers are together, fragrance "bursts" rather than being scattered.

In Chapter III this technique was termed "transitional metaphor" because it creates much the same impact as does metaphor. The reader is forced to provide his own "meaning," his own transition for the sections as they appear, just as in metaphor he must complete or at least recognize the suggested relationship. In poems like "A Widow's Lament" and "Love Song" the position of images is nearly as important as their content. This principle of organization is central to many of Williams' poetic techniques, providing as it does the basis of structure for many poems throughout his career.

Montage, for example, is one variation of juxtaposition. Single elements are arranged to create a complex scene in accurate perspective. Each detail is listed separately, with no explanation for its position and no transition connecting it with other images:

```
    ...              One
black (of course, red)
rose; a fat old woman backing
through a screen door. Two,
from the armpits
down, contrasting in bed,
breathless; a letter from
a ship; leaves filling,
making, a tree ...
```
            ("A Place (Any Place) To Transcend All Places,"
                                          CLP, p. 113.)

The effectiveness of what Williams called "a fascinating sort of composition" is derived from the presentation of details without comment: "nothing 'about' the subject, a bare placing of the matter before the attention, as an object, that which with wit a man might see for himself—swiftly and to the point."[2] By eliminating slowing transitions, the poet can achieve what Williams called "the white light" of perception, an almost instantaneous poetic "apprehension":[3]

> The shell flowers
> the wax grapes and peaches
> the fancy oak or mahogany tables
> the highbacked baronial chairs
>
> Or the girls' legs
> agile stanchions
> the breasts
> the pinheads . . .
>
> Then unexpectedly
> a small house with a soaring oak
> leafless above it
>
> Someone should summarize these things
> in the interest of local
> government or how
> a spotted dog goes up a gutter— . . .
>   ("11/10," *CEP*, pp. 309-310.)

Through this series of vignettes, Williams creates a definite conclusion as he "summarizes these things." The effectiveness of the local scene, however, is derived from the total cumulative structure rather than from individual figures. Each image helps to create the whole impression, but its meaning in the entire composite is often very different from that in isolation. Williams depended heavily on *montage* as an organizational principle during the nineteen-twenties and thirties, using it as the rationale for later more complicated structures.

That the effects of this technique were far-reaching is evident in his 1956 praise of René Char for his achievement of "cumulative interest":

> once he gets the theme he follows it in example after example with telling effect until gradually it becomes clear by the sheer persistence of what he has to say. It is a perfectly legitimate device of the artist and increases the pleasure of the reader by piling up the emphasis with variations of detail until the total effect is overwhelming.[4]

Perhaps the late principle of organization most dependent on the single phrase or detail is that of "words, rhythmically organized" which Williams defended in a television interview:

Q.   ... here's part of a poem you yourself have written: . . . "2 partridges/ 2 mallard ducks/ a Dungeness crab/ 24 hours out/ of the Pacific/ and 2 live-frozen/ trout/ from Denmark . . ." Now, that sounds just like a fashionable grocery list!

A.   It is a fashionable grocery list.

Q.   Well—is it poetry?

A.   We poets have to talk in a language which is not English. It is the American idiom. Rhythmically it's organized as a sample of the American idiom. It has as much originality as jazz. If you say "2 partridges, 2 mallard ducks, a Dungeness crab"— if you treat that rhythmically, ignoring the practical sense it forms a jagged pattern. It is, to my mind, poetry . . . .

Q.   But shouldn't a word mean something when you see it?

A.   In prose, an English word means what it says. In poetry, you're listening to two things   . . .   you're listening to the sense, the common sense of what it says. But it says more. That is the difficulty.[5]

Williams early recognized the need for rhythmic arrangements of words and for structures that could contain complex subjects while at the same time moving fast enough to hold a reader's attention. Achieving a structure which satisfied these requirements, however, took many years of experimentation, experimentation which was put to the test of use only when Williams' subject matter became correspondingly complex. Structure was no problem until he began writing *Paterson* in the early forties.

To arrive at a satisfactory epic structure, Williams had to pass through his period of greatest transition. The tenets of Objectivism had dominated his poetry for fifteen years. The fact that Objectivism allowed as subject only the concrete "thing" (presented literally and in isolation from even the poet) gradually drove Williams into stalemate and then into change as he realized that he was ignoring more of the local than he had included. In the late thirties, Williams decided that what he needed was to modify his definition of both the poem and the role of the poet.

Still maintaining that the poem was to re-create the local, Williams now saw that it must present a complex view rather than a simple one. It must include many components of life: the poet and his perception, the subject and its surroundings, related objects in the fabric of life. In short, Williams felt that the poet must take the details of his observation and combine them into a meaningful whole. Man observes; the poet interprets the observation and relates it to life. And he cannot suppress or exclude his own reactions: they are an integral part of his local, probably the part he knows best. As Williams wrote in 1947, "The objective in writing is, to reveal. It is not to teach, not to advertise, not to sell, not even to communicate (for that needs two) but to reveal, which needs no other than the man himself. . . ."[6]

Once Williams began writing the epic which would present life "whole," he found that many changes in technique were necessary. His new point of view forced him back to an even wider acceptance of figures of speech, now useful in presenting thought sequences and abstractions. The increased scope of the poem also necessitated more connective figures—symbolic metaphor as well as transitional. And, in structure, the self-determined forms of the previous limited poems could not carry the multiple segments of the new, particularly not of the epic.

Rather than evolve a definite formula for structure, however, Williams continued to rely on his faith in language and in experimentation: "In my mind, all along, I was disturbed as to how I would put the thing [Paterson] down on the page. Finally I let form take care of itself; the colloquial language, my own language, set the pace."[7] With Williams following the demands of language, line and stanza were largely self determined. And for structural format, he returned to the only expansive techniques he had—those of transitional metaphor and montage—and to a new concept of structure, that of design. As he wrote metaphorically in the opening of his 1948 The Clouds:

> In the bare trees old husks make new designs
> Love moves the crows before the dawn
> The cherry sun ushers in a new phase . . .

It is precisely the "old husks" of objective description and the "new phase" of more figurative subjectivity which form the "new designs" of these poems. Williams' reaction against the single image viewed in isolation is evident in his comment from "Tribute to the Painters":

> there came to me
>   just now
>   the knowledge of
> the tyranny of the image
>   and how
>   men
> in their designs
>   have learned
>   to shatter it . . .
>
>   (*Pictures*, p. 137.)

Static representations of objects are no longer valid; only when fitted with other components in a design of total life does the image have a part.

2.

OF all Williams' poetry, *Paterson* is the best illustration of his concept of design and of his reliance on figurative speech; not only is the entire poem a single metaphor, but it also depends for much of its structure on symbolic and transitional metaphors. The epic itself was, of course, responsible for Williams' new concern with structure: its length and diversity forced him to find a flexible design, and in so doing, to leave one of his former artistic beliefs—that of chronology as organizational principle. Faced with the complexity of the man-city-river-art which Paterson is, Williams realized that "consecutiveness" might well be secondary. He turned instead to a spatial arrangement which he described in 1945 as putting "designs" of color on a blank wall, "moving about . . . until at the end the meaning would be totally revealed."[8] That he saw metaphor as the means of approaching such design is evident in his comment that "one extended metaphor freely handled" would allow the poet "SPACE, within the metaphor, to maneuver, to go about at will."[9]

Paterson is consequently the complete expression of Williams' extended-metaphor technique. The "design" of the poem comprises the poet's intimate interpretations of life, made concrete through images, scenes, events, and characters—all elements juxtaposed without conventional time sequence and, for the most part, without transitions. Williams provides what coherence is necessary through transitional and symbolic metaphors connecting the sharply defined images, all now arranged in a type of theme-and-variation structure, as these few lines from the epic indicate:

> Even during the Revolution Hamilton had been impressed by the site of the Great Falls of the Passaic . . . . Here was water-power to turn the mill wheels and the navigable river to carry manufactured goods to the market centers: a national manufactury . . . .
>
> Give up my money! . . .
>
> That would be a hard thing
> for me to do. What would my rich friends say? . . . .
>
> The beauty of holiness,
> if this it be,
> is the only beauty
> visible in this place
> other than the view
> and a fresh budding tree.
>
> So I started to get rid of my money. It didn't take
> me long I can tell you! I threw it away with both
> hands. And I began to feel better . . . .
>
> —and leaned on the parapet, thinking
> From here, one could see him—that
> tied man, that cold blooded
> murderer . April! in the distance
> being hanged. Groups at various
> vantages along the cliff . having
> gathered since before daybreak
> to witness it.
>
> One kills
> for money but doesn't always get it . . . .
>
> . . . . The prominent purpose of the Society
>
> was the manufacture of cotton goods.
>
> (*Paterson* II, ii, pp. 87-91.)

Organization here depends on transitional metaphor or juxtaposition of recurring themes. The placing of the strophe concerning Judas ("that cold blooded/ murderer") between the testimonial of the man who became poor in order to live and the comment describing society's materialism adds emphasis to each image. The larger themes—industry and money as the core of society, the contrast between society and nature (and natural man), the correlation between renouncing monetary values and "the beauty of holiness"—are vividly presented through the interaction of the prose text concerning Hamilton, the narration of Klaus Ehrens, and the comments of the poet.

Omnipresent irony builds from the first mention of Hamilton's plans for "a national manufactury" (the Hamilton who, one remembers, considered the American people "a great beast") to the realization that the Paterson area has evolved as Hamilton's concern had indicated—much industry but little humanity. "The prominent purpose of the Society," it is evident, is not "holiness."

These motifs, of course, interrelate with those in other parts of the poem to provide richer implications than these few lines can show. Because of the recurrence of allusions to images as well as of the images themselves in the motif pattern, many assume qualities of "symbolic metaphor": they have no exact, definable meaning but they do carry multiple suggestions, as do "fresh budding tree" and "April" in this passage.

Organization remains generally uniform throughout the five books of *Paterson*, but verbal technique varies. In fact, Williams employed devices throughout *Paterson* in approximately the same sequence as he had throughout the continuum of his poetry.

In the first book, published in 1946, the speaker presents external descriptions, phrased both literally and figuratively and interspersed with expressions of subjective feelings. Abstractions are reinforced with concrete detail:

> a bud forever green,
> tight-curled, upon the pavement, perfect
> in juice and substance but divorced, divorced
> from its fellows, fallen low—
>
> Divorce is
> the sign of knowledge in our time,
> divorce! divorce!

(I, ii, p. 28.)

With Book II in 1948 Williams presented one inclusive scene both objectively and metaphorically, with attention shifting to *per-*

sonae other than the poet. Characteristic of his use of motion to define life, Williams here personified natural objects while picturing common man as inanimate: "Thickets gather about groups of squat sand-pine, ... roots, for the most part, writhing/upon the surface" contrasts with "benches on which/a few children have been propped by the others .... Three middle aged men with iron smiles."

The poet left objective description for more nearly symbolic representation in Book III, working out his concepts through images of wind, fire, and water:

> Fire burns; that is the first law.
> When a wind fans it the flames
>
> are carried abroad. Talk
> fans the flames. They have
>
> manoeuvred it so that to write
> is a fire and not only of the blood.
>
> (III, ii, p. 137.)

The prose within this book also relates to these symbolic motifs.

In Book IV Williams, attempting to provide more exact answers, finally realized that external details alone are inadequate, as are symbolic representations. Thus he turned to the total complex scene. Instead of presenting characters externally, he revealed them participating in intimate acts. The ironic "idyl" among Phyllis, Corydon, and Paterson presents the characters in the best dramatic format:

Corydon & Phyllis
> Good morning, Phyllis. You are beautiful this morning (in a common sort of way) I wonder if you know how lovely you really are, Phyllis, my little Milk Maid (That's good! The lucky man!) I dreamt of you last night.

.

A Letter
> I don't care what you say. Unless Mother writes me, herself, that you've stopped drinking—and I mean *stopped drinking*—I won't come home.

.

Corydon & Phyllis
> What sort of people do you come from, Phyllis?

> My father's a drunk.
> That's more humility than the situation demands.
> Never be ashamed of your origins.
>
> I'm not. It's just the truth . . . .
>
> (IV, i, pp. 185-186.)

Although the poet is withdrawn during the dramatic presentation, he reappears throughout the rest of the book to make personal comments in a calmly authoritative tone. The situations which he presents are personal, but he is no longer self-conscious.

Like his progression from a simple view of life to a complex one, Dr. Williams moved from small images to entire scenes and—in perception—from the physical world to a composite of the physical, mental, and ritualistic. In 1958 the fifth book of *Paterson* continued his progression into a world more symbolic than literal, the immensities of existence better depicted through figurative language than through any medium Williams had yet used.

> . . . the Unicorn
> is penned by a low
> wooden fence
> in April!
> the same month
> when at the foot of the post
> he saw the man dig up
> the red snake
> and kill it with a spade . . . .
>
> The (self) direction has been changed
> the serpent
> its tail in its mouth
> "the river has returned to its beginnings"
> and backward
> (and forward)
> it tortures itself within me
> until time has been washed finally under . . . .
>
> (V, iii, pp. 270-271.)

The unity of Book V stems from the central image of the tapestry, "The Hunt of the Unicorn"; from a focus more limited than in earlier books; and from clearer transitions. In the above excerpt, for example, the mention of April, the unicorn, and the snake suggests

Williams' increasing preoccupation with timelessness, infinity, and God. Through figurative transitions and symbols, the whole book treats of actual experiences and people in the mythic framework of the tapestry and its associated themes. It consequently permits Williams to express his views of man, art, life, and death—the deepest issues accessible to the poet.

Because *Paterson* V was not originally included in the epic format and did not appear until seven years after Book IV, the first four books were naturally judged as the completed work. Critical opinion about the four-volume epic, however, was divided: because technique and style varied throughout, appraisal of the whole was difficult. Hurt deeply by what appeared to be critical rejection on the basis of "formlessness," Dr. Williams replied despairingly, "Christ! Are there no intelligent men in the world?"[10]

Then, although he tried to continue his prolific production in order to clarify his artistic position, Williams was slowed by the first of a series of strokes. The following year, 1951, he commented that he wanted desperately to be understood, that he had to express "the facts of the situation which can no longer be delayed":

> I must now, in other words, make myself clear. I must gather together the stray ends of what I have been thinking and make my full statement as to their meaning or quit.[11]

The results of this urgency to make a "full statement" are the poems of the next decade that appear in *The Desert Music, Journey to Love,* and *Paterson* V.

3.

THESE volumes create a magnificent description of the poet's consciousness through first person point of view, personal reminiscence, colloquial and metaphoric language, and Williams' adroit speech line. Any one of the poems illustrates the interaction of the subject, detailed and actual in its own right, and the poet's reactions to it and other objects, all culminating in a rich, comprehensive statement: "order" evolving from the minutiae of objective and subjective "fact."

The Desert Music is Williams' full statement of poetic theory illustrated through accurate details of experience, stressing the

themes of design, imagination, invention, and the identity of the
poet. Yet none of these poems is "abstract" or "didactic" because
the theory grows from factual detail. "To a Dog Injured in the Street"
shows Williams using experience as a means to valid generalizations,
with literal description evolving from or culminating in the figures
of speech which reveal the poet's feelings:

> It is myself,
>> not the poor beast lying there
>>> yelping with pain
> that brings me to myself with a start—
>> as at the explosion
>>> of a bomb, a bomb that has laid
> all the world waste.
>> I can do nothing
>>> but sing about it . . . .
>
> I remember Norma
>> our English setter of my childhood
>>> her silky ears
> and expressive eyes . . . .
> I remember also
>> a dead rabbit
>>> lying harmlessly
> on the outspread palm
>> of a hunter's hand . . . .
>
> (*Pictures,* pp. 86-87.)

These memories culminate finally in the poet's declaration of his
belief in "the power of beauty/ to right all wrongs," a figure which
caps the series of literal descriptions and echoes the opening implication. This poem shares with much of Williams' late work the schema
of progression described by Frederick Eckman: "Though . . . the
poem usually clings tight to the concrete reality of its subject . . .
some of its more exploratory efforts gradually abandon concrete for
abstract, specific for general, by a progression curiously like that of
inductive logic."[12]

In moving toward a highly polished design which interrelates
many areas of experience and emotion, Williams often used transitional or symbolic metaphor. The poet still viewed figures of speech
with suspicion, however, as this excerpt from "Shadows" indicates:

Right and left
    climb the ladders of night
        as dawn races
to put out the stars.
    That
        is the poetic figure
but we know
    better; . . .

                    (*Pictures,* p. 150.)

Figures of speech may lend vividness to reality but they cannot distort the actual because men will not accept such tampering: "we know/ better." The figurative expression used in these poems is again primarily symbolic or transitional, serving structural purposes as well as linguistic ones.

Journey to Love continues the interwoven structure, the themes now of love rather than of poetic principles, or at times of the two combined. Technically, many poems of the two volumes are similar, except that some of those in the 1955 volume are again descriptive. Dealing with what appear to be Dr. Williams' personal observations, they are more subjective than the early poems of description but less introspective than those of pure comment. In these poems Williams uses literal expression chiefly in descriptive areas and figurative expression in subjective ones.

The descriptive poems also differ in structure. Being shorter, they proceed either *from* a figure of speech or down *to* a concluding figure, with the body of the poem devoted to the central presentation. Williams here uses the single image presented fully rather than the *montage* or transitional metaphor.

Nearly all the poems of the 1962 *Pictures from Brueghel* illustrate the same techniques. Style is partially determined by the poet's role: here he is an observer but not an objective one. He writes of local scenes, art objects, and people dear to him, approaching each with unfeigned naturalness. There is much first-person comment; as he writes about a postcard, nothing is easier than to begin (as he does), "In my hand I hold/ a postcard." The stanza pattern of tercets can also be considered natural for Williams. Similar to early structures, it is shorter and more immediate than the triadic stanza, consistent with the poet's preference for a short, abrupt impression.

Language—both literal and figurative—is simple, again the norm for Williams. As the *persona* in many of these late poems, he expresses his feelings directly: "it is a satisfaction," "I love myself more," "Sick as I am." In this final acceptance of his own emotion, the poet needed no rhetoric. Those figures of speech used are the familiar ones of personification, metaphor, colloquial figures. Transitional figures are largely unnecessary because of the poems' brevity and more limited subject matter.

Some of these last poems have no figures of speech at all; others employ those so natural that they fit readily into Williams' ideal poetic vocabulary, the common idiom. "Iris" illustrates figurative language used for both thematic and structural effect within the shorter poem:

> a burst of iris so that
> come down for
> breakfast
>
> we searched through the
> rooms for
> that
>
> sweetest odor . . .

Beginning figuratively for emphasis, Williams phrases his reaction in simple colloquial terms, even to "come down for/ breakfast." The vehemence of the opening is caught and intensified twice figuratively in the concluding lines, lines also essential to visual description:

> . . . a blue as
> of the sea
> struck
>
> startling us from among
> those trumpeting
> petals

(Pictures, p. 30.)

No word or figure which seems unnatural for the poet is used here.

The question of structure arises often in relation to these short last poems. In fact, some critics tend to dismiss them as "insignificant" because they are short, because Williams had abandoned the triadic line. Just as with every technical change Williams made, there is reason for this one.

Intention must be one consideration in judging any poem. After his 1951 resolution to make clear his ideas, Williams had written poems of more complete expression and more detailed illustration than any others of his career—those of *The Desert Music* and *Journey to Love*. After such explicit statement, he returned to his more characteristic indirect presentation with this 1960 comment: "sometimes when I write I don't want to say anything. I just want to present it."[13]

Because Williams considered poetry similar to painting in many respects, his seeking a kindred technique in graphic art is not surprising. For several decades, he had admired the interwoven design of the tapestry, each figure meaningful in itself yet of even more significance in relation to the whole. This pattern (of particularly the Flemish tapestry "The Hunt of the Unicorn") had a strong influence on Williams' poems of the mid-fifties and on his concept of the triadic line. (In fact, he had probably been trying to achieve an interwoven effect in *Paterson*, although the abruptness of that earlier sectional approach had resulted in a design more like a patchwork quilt than a tapestry.) The attraction of the latter, as Williams wrote, stemmed from its perfect unity, details woven "all together" just as are the details of life when viewed by the poet's imagination.

However desirable such unity was, no tapestry could include all of life; subjects must somewhere be limited, just as are those of Williams' last poems. Having investigated the possibilities of tapestry as design, he turned to the portrait, which he considered the best means to "a new continent" in art. The portrait as Williams conceived it could objectively reveal the artist himself, "the hidden work of his own imagination; what he is." In such an art form, the artist must include his subject in all its complexity, himself and his reactions to the subject, the environment of both. In short, Williams saw the portrait as a vehicle for many "varieties of experience."[14] And of all the art that might be considered a kind of portraiture, he turned to that of Pieter Brueghel. Williams' aim in his poems was similar to Brueghel's in his paintings: to re-create his personal local, particularly its human elements; to do so with sensitivity and accuracy; and to use technical mastery to achieve dynamic presentations rather than static ones (see Brueghel's painting "The Kermess" and Williams' poem "The Dance").

Williams' transfer of interest from the tapestry to Brueghel's grimly humorous paintings of individual scenes necessarily changed the appearance of his poems. Intensity of focus shortened the poem so that the wide triadic line was disproportionate. The resulting tercet arrangement gave a more definite shape to the poem, suggesting the rigid outlines of an object.

The similarity between the shape of "Iris" and a painting is obvious. The poem is complete on one page. Its orderly stanza arrangement provides balance. Line enjambment is intensified by the absence of punctuation—the eye moves so rapidly from line to line following the run-on sentence pattern that the impression is one of wholeness, in shape and in time. Reaction to the poem is consequently visual. Design still dominates the reader's impression, but a design perhaps more natural to hurried contemporary times than that of the tapestry because it is shorter and more easily grasped. Yet, for all the brevity and subject limitation of these 1962 poems, they encompass wide ranges of feeling and experience, chiefly because of Williams' masterful employment of figurative language. As a result, the designs of most of these last poems continue to be based on figures of speech.

Even this necessarily summary view of Williams' poetry has shown that figurative language, especially metaphor, was of major significance throughout the poet's career. In his use of it as both structural and verbal device, it dominated the style and structure of many of his poems. After surveying Williams' poetry and theory, one can only add as a postscript to those who consider his work devoid of figurative speech that, if Williams ever had "shed" figurative language "as a snake sheds its skin," then, equally snakelike, he had grown a second skin of even greater strength and beauty.

William Carlos Williams may well have been a poet "without decoration," but he was seldom "without metaphor."

CHAPTER FIVE

"The Melody Line Is Everything"

1.

JUST as Dr. Williams' theory of poetic language was based on the American idiom, so was his concept of "measure," his term for the rhythmic pattern of the poem. Williams believed that standard meters were invalid because they had grown from speech rhythms now decadent. The accurate poet therefore had to break with prescribed accent patterns and create new measures which reflected living, contemporary speech. As he announced in 1953:

> The iamb is not the normal measure of American speech. The foot has to be expanded or contracted in terms of actual speech. The key to modern poetry is *measure*, which must reflect the flux of modern life. You should find a variable measure for the fixed.[1]

Williams' theory of "variability" was his answer to the classic poetic problem of maintaining order while re-creating the unpredictable movement of life within art objects. Because he felt that a basic order was essential, he had balked at *vers libre:* "You can't be completely free because you will have lost measure. And the only thing a man can do with his life is to measure it."[2] Disdainful of this rationale which dominated much poetry of the early twentieth century, he was forced to rely on his single principle of prosody, that measure was to reflect the rhythms of contemporary American speech, a speech which had its own particular stability. Working from this general concept, however, Williams experimented for forty years before attaining the balance between regularity and freedom which he felt necessary to poetic measure.

Dr. Williams began, as any artist must, by imitating traditional forms, but his experimentation within them soon made his unrest evident. In the 1909 "To His Lady" he mixed a standard accent pattern with lines phrased in near-speech rhythms: "Love, change thy name; Elizabeth/ Is apter far. For then a breath/ Could smoothly ride it." In other early poems he did not hesitate to interrupt regular rhythmic patterns, as the awkward irregularities of "A Street Market, New York, 1908" show.

Poems labeled "1910–1912" in the unpublished typescripts at the State University of New York at Buffalo show Williams replacing conventional stanza patterns with structures which grew from combinations of individual lines. Length of line appears to be determined by unit of thought, a key technique in later work. "And Thus with All Praise" also anticipated Pound's injunction to "compose in the sequence of the musical phrase":

> Wonderful creatures!
> Why must I call you bride and mother?
> Curst be the idle mockery and fashion lie of such names!
> Be delight unto me rather!
> Joy at the encounter!
> Sorrow at the ends of things
> Be to me deeds of compassion:
> Have these for name, none other.

As early as 1913 Williams' critical comments show his concern with the need for a new basis of rhythm. In March of that year he argued with Harriet Monroe over what she had considered "irregular" measure in his poem "Immortal":

> As to the meter . . . if you wish to judge it as a fixed iambic measure you are dogmatically right as to the disturbing fourth and sixth lines; but why not call it some other kind of a measure?[3]

As his statement illustrates, Williams was dissatisfied with "fixed measure"; but, as the poem itself shows, he found escaping from standard accent patterns difficult. Aside from some inversion and the two lines to which Miss Monroe objected, the poem moves in fairly regular iambic rhythms, just as does much of his early work. Although he was "positively repelled by the old order," Williams still demanded regularity: "I wanted order, which I appreciated. The orderliness of verse appealed to me—as it must to any man—but even more I wanted a new order."[4] His letters to Miss Monroe show also that he was studying other poets' techniques; he used as justification for breaking metric "rules" the fact that Yeats often dropped the last syllable of a three-syllable foot.[5] At this time his approach in finding a new meter was to modify traditional forms rather than to create his own.

So far as innovation was concerned, Williams' prosodic experimentation between 1909 and 1920 centered chiefly in line arrangement, a device he found invaluable as a guide to reading and interpretation. When Miss Monroe changed one of his poems before publishing it in *Poetry,* Williams reacted angrily: "It will be physically impossible for anyone to guess how I intended it to be read the way you have rearranged matters."[6] In *I Wanted to Write a Poem* he recalled that even during these early years his rationale of line arrangement—"the rhythmic unit"—was of more significance than any formal accent scheme:

> The rhythmic unit decided the form of my poetry. When I came to the end of a rhythmic unit (not necessarily a sentence) I ended the line. . . . The rhythmic unit usually came to me in a lyrical outburst. I wanted it to look that way on the page. I didn't go in for long lines because of my nervous nature. I couldn't. The rhythmic pace was the pace of speech, an excited pace. . . . The lines were short, *not* studied (p. 15).

Line arrangement was Williams' means of determining structure as well as of indicating rhythm; early experiments show that poetic form was of great interest to him. He used the refrain ingeniously to provide structural format; he also at times relied on formal and elaborate stanza patterns. By 1915, however, he had discovered the "paragraph" organization: if the poem was to represent the poet's thought on one subject, one stanza should suffice.

This change was significant to Williams' prosody: free from preconceived stanza demands, he could use lines of any length in any arrangement. He could also substitute the conventions of conversation for those of poetry and thus stay within an "orderly" and meaningful discipline. "Portrait of a Lady" illustrates his use of mock conversation in dialogue, here between the hesitating, self-conscious romantic and his antagonistically literal other self:

> Your thighs are appletrees
> whose blossoms touch the sky.

Which sky? The sky
where Watteau hung a lady's
slipper. Your knees
are a southern breeze—or
a gust of snow. Agh! what
sort of man was Fragonard?
—as if that answered
anything. Ah, yes—below
the knees, since the tune
drops that way, it is
one of those white summer days,
the tall grass of your ankles
flickers upon the shore—
Which shore?—
the sand clings to my lips—
Which shore?
Agh, petals maybe. How
should I know?
Which shore? Which shore?
I said petals from an appletree.

(*CEP*, p. 40.)

As well as achieving irony, the question device allows much freedom
of rhythm in that questions require answers. Because the *personae*
involved will express themselves differently, the rhythms of the poem
will vary. Here, the romantic speaker's gradual change in tone creates
even more variation in pace. He answers immediately after the first
question, or so the position of "The sky" suggests. The increased
frequency of dashes, however, implies that he requires more time for
thought, harassed as he is both by the abrupt questions and by his
own inarticulateness. After a halting return to the subject with "Ah,
yes," he makes a valiant attempt to finish, but his phrases shorten
with his patience and he turns for refuge to his first successful line.

Williams could have achieved a strong iambic measure by arranging the line in longer units, as for example:

Your thighs are apple trees whose blossoms touch the sky;
Your knees a southern breeze or gust of snow.

The line arrangement in the finished poem, however, breaks the
pattern convincingly; not only are the lines divided, they also are
interspersed with metrically abrupt segments, "Which sky?" "Agh,"

"Ah, yes." The poet resumes his description in lines of near-anapestic measure: "since the tune/ drops that way, it is/ one of those white summer days,/ the tall grass of your ankles/ flickers upon the shore—" but again regularity disappears into fragmentary conversation. The half-assumed meter only adds to the poem's irony, just as does the figurative language. Both the traditional meter and the diction of a love poem have been burlesqued.

In the poems of *Al Que Quiere*, 1917, Williams continued to duplicate natural speech situations. He used direct address in over half the poems and a first-person narrative focus in 90 per cent. Even the few portraits are monologues so that the characters speak in their own idioms. He apparently found the natural line easier to achieve in poems of believable speech situations, and therefore used such devices until he grew more confident of rhythms themselves.

In fact, all parts of these 1917 poems reflect the conventions of speech: stanzas are based on the paragraphing of conversation, and capitalization and punctuation mark off complete sentences or thought units rather than arbitrary lines.

"The Old Men" illustrates Williams' use of speech conventions as well as his skill in direct address:

> Old men who have studied
> every leg show
> in the city . . .

Beginning with a simple cognitive statement, Williams moves into more subjective description in the next section of address:

> Old men cut from touch
> by the perfumed music—
> polished or fleeced skulls
> that stand before
> the whole theater
> in silent attitudes
> of attention,—

and finally into a third address which gives the old men "precedence" over "dark-faced/ husbands whose minds/ are a street with arc-lights." Although he ends this third section of address with a period, Williams has as yet made no statement to the old men; that is to come after still another opening:

Solitary old men for whom
we find no excuses—
I bow my head in shame
for those who malign you.
Old men
the peaceful beer of impotence
be yours!

(*CEP*, p. 158.)

With all but two lines involved in direct address, the sections of
apostrophe provide structure for the poem. The first three phrases
build to a climax in both motion and content with the arc-light
figure, aided by unconventional use of punctuation and capitalization.
By placing a capitalized word after an open line (11. 3 and 4),
Williams connects the first phrase of address with the second, even
while maintaining their distinctness. The comma-dash punctuation
at the end of the second phrase indicates that descriptions are to fuse
so that motion continues to the period. The poet then begins again,
adding *Solitary* to the epithet for emphasis. Following his own simple
statement, he concludes with the fifth section of address and its
masterful metaphor.

The movement of this poem depends primarily on punctuation,
the dash used in conjunction with the open line. Only three lines end
with a period or exclamation point. Such use of punctuation is necessary because most of these lines are syntactically end-stopped. In his
relatively early poems Williams experimented noticeably with devices
which control movement. In "Good Night," for example, he uses
end-stopped lines to depict sequential actions and enjambment to
describe concurrent happenings. Here syntax halts motion at the end
of each line:

In brilliant gas light
I turn the kitchen spigot
and watch the water plash
into the clean white sink . . .

Later in the poem Williams creates a feeling of simultaneity by using
enjambment. He forces meaning to continue by placing conjunctions
at the ends of lines and by separating subjects from verbs, objects
from prepositions:

it is
memory playing the clown—
three vague, meaningless girls
full of smells and
the rustling sounds of
cloth rubbing on cloth and
little slippers on carpet—

(*CEP*, p. 145.)

So far as Williams' line itself is concerned, it has often been referred to as "two-stress," a reasonable term when critics and readers (and poets) were accustomed to looking for accent patterns. In this terminology, most of his lines written in the twenties are two-stress with single-stress lines for variation. The important quality about such a stress pattern, however, is that it is by no means regular, nor are the stresses of equal intensity. In fact, any exacting pattern appears to exist only in the critics' minds.

The following lines can be considered two-stress:

In brilliant gas light
I turn the kitchen spigot
and watch the water plash
into the clean white sink.

These lines, however, can also be read as phrases, accented lightly on all key words:

In brilliant gas light
I turn the kitchen spigot
and watch the water plash
into the clean white sink.

One hearing Williams read his poems would be inclined to adopt the second accent pattern, for he gave little variation to accents unless punctuation occurred. Most accents fall on substantives; heavy stresses are rare. He read most lines as units, rapidly, with pauses following each. When lines enjamb, however—as do the first four of this approximation of Williams reading "Fish"—he emphasized the meaning of the section rather than of each line:

It is the whales | that drive
the small fish | into the fiords. |
I have seen | forty or fifty
of them | in the water at one time. |
I have been | in a little boat |
when the water was boiling |
on all sides of us |
from them swimming underneath. ||[7]

(*CEP*, p. 177.)

2.

IN the poems of the twenties and thirties Williams continued to use enjambment, capitalization, and punctuation to indicate thought divisions. One significant advance in these poems is that he no longer relied on direct address or first person conventions; he used the natural speech line without pretense, and therefore was free again to experiment.

Dominant structures changed with each volume of poems. In the early twenties, Williams combined couplets and tercets into single stanzas:

My wife's new pink slippers
have gay pom-poms.
There is not a spot or a stain
on their satin toes or their sides.
All night they lie together
under her bed's edge . . .

("The Thinker," *CEP*, p. 220.)

Later, he broke the masses into separate units:

a woman in blue

who was laughing and
leaning forward to look up

into the man's half
averted face

and a boy of eight who was
looking at the middle of

the man's belly
at a watchchain—
                    ("The Right of Way," *CEP*, p. 258.)

This relatively long section can easily be read without a pause, achieving simultaneity of scene. The structure is also interesting as an unconscious foreshadowing of Williams' later technique of dividing one line into its component feet; whereas these lines have two segments, later lines have three.

Williams recalled of his poetry in the twenties that, in addition to being interested in regular groupings of lines, he was intent on concentration, "getting rid of redundancies . . . trying to make it go faster."[8] This tightening of structure is one of three main techniques which guided his experimentation during his half-century of poetry. His own description of the poetic process shows that he put words down as they came to him and then shaped them into the finished poem, condensing and interrelating. This approach was particularly noticeable in the poems of the late nineteen-twenties and thirties when short vignettes, focused on single details, dominated his poetic mode.

These years comprise Williams' Objectivist period, a period chiefly important to prosody in its emphasis on the "shape" of the poem. Objectivism considered each poem autonomous and unique, and therefore deserving of its own form. During these years, Williams attempted to create individual structures for each poem. Such typography as that used in "Perpetuum Mobile: The City," while never typical of his work, did occur:

                    — a dream
         we dreamed
                    each
         separately
                    we two —
                              (*CEP*, p. 384.)

The form of Williams' short Objectivist poems seems to have been determined by individual lines rather than by formal stanza arrangements:

Monday
        the canna flaunts
its crimson head

crimson lying folded
crisply down upon

                the invisible . . .
                        ("10/10," *CEP*, p. 299.)

Another innovation, justifiable if extraneous parts were to be elimi-
nated from the poem, was the incorporation of the title as first line:

"The Yachts"

contend in a sea . . .

The change most important to Williams' later work, however, was
that in line length. Previously he had used lines as guides to meaning,
creating effects through arrangement and enjambment. Now line
length *per se* became of interest: descriptions required short phrases
("On hot days/ the sewing machine/ whirling") while more reflective
content fell into longer lines ("What chance have the old?/ There are
no duties for them.")

Once Williams had focused his attention on the individual line,
a myriad of structural possibilities opened before him. The poems of
the early forties show wide variation in both line and stanza. He
wrote in three-, four-, five-, six-, and nine-line stanzas; sonnets; couplets; and verse paragraphs; using short and long lines in each structure. Of all his stanza and line combinations, it is the verse paragraph
that dominates his work of this decade—probably because the absence
of formal pattern gives each line maximum freedom, as this excerpt
from "To All Gentleness" illustrates:

                        money,
        articulated to government mounts still
        as wonder in the minds of the speculators,

        to buy
                (the ferment wedging their skulls
        even wider)

                        to buy, shall we say, the
        grass, or a small cloud perhaps . . .
                        (*CLP*, p. 25.)

There are obvious dangers inherent in the verse paragraph structure. The poet must rely on his own sense of proportion, his own ear, to determine the effectiveness of each line and its position in the complete poem. And while such a form has freedom, it lacks the musical regularity Williams demanded. His final solution in structure led him through more prosodic experimentation in the coming fifteen years than he had attempted in the previous thirty-five.

3.

AT the close of the nineteen-thirties, then, Williams had thrown off what he considered the restrictions of both traditional rhythms and traditional stanza arrangements. He was consequently forced to create new meters and structures to replace those he had cast aside. One technical principal which proved especially valuable in his coming invention was that of what he termed "the auditory quality." Williams believed he could reach a new auditory effect by assimilating relevant characteristics of music into his poetry. Coupling the two arts was, of course, not new; but Williams followed his theory with his usual perseverance until he found successful means of implementing it. What he was aiming for was a "metric structure" in which grammatical units are ignored and "the progression goes over into the next bar as much as the musical necessity requires . . . a sequence of musical bars arranged vertically on the page, and capable of infinite modulation."[9]

In his search for basic regularity combined with speech freedom, Williams used a wide variety of lines and stanzas, most of which failed to strike the dynamic balance he required. Often the poems of the early forties are strange mixtures of freedom and order; having found no single form which would embody both qualities, Williams moved from one pattern to the other by section. Although the short poems are interesting in their great variety, Williams' technical progress during this decade is best seen in the books of *Paterson*. Rather than serving as the culmination of Williams' poetic technique, the epic became instead the proving ground for his most valuable prosodic experiments.

As he wrote in 1947, "I am trying in *Paterson* to work out the problems of a new prosody."[10] And he later recalled:

I had to invent my form, if form it was. . . . I knew I had what I
wanted to say. I knew that I wanted to say it in *my* form. I was
aware that it wasn't a finished form, yet I knew it was not form-
less.[11]

Dr. Williams' theoretical statements at this time were of necessity
general; when he began working with the epic, he knew only what he
did *not* want. His procedure, then, was to innovate continuously,
discarding some results, incorporating others into his later style. The
various books of the epic, taken in sequence, chronicle the stylistic
changes of the period. Books I and II are relatively similar; Books
III and IV differ greatly from each other, from earlier books, and
from Book V. The progression of metric technique within *Paterson*
is generally from the obvious to the subtle, from the cluttered to the
simple, and from the needlessly free to the flexible yet orderly.

Book I is noticeable for consistent form. Only one section of the
poem falls into quatrains or tercets—the rest is arranged in the
familiar verse paragraph, each long line broken by the modern-day
caesura employed frequently by Williams:*

> And there, against him, stretches the low mountain.
> The Park's her head, carved, above the Falls, by the quiet
> river . . . .
> Pearls at her ankles, her monstrous hair
> spangled with apple-blossoms is scattered about into
> the back-country, waking their dreams—where the deer run
> and the wood-duck nests protecting his gallant plumage.
> (I, i, p. 17.)

In later passages within the first book, the stanza form appears to
grow irregular because Williams uses isolated lines and short phrases
within the strophe. He is, however, only separating lines from the
standard form for emphasis, using vertical space rather than punctuation as a guide to meaning:

> while the
> currents float still in mid-air, to
> fall—

---

* As Williams wrote in approximately 1947, the caesura offered him
"the greatest hope I have discovered so far for a study of the modern
line; . . . The caesura to take the place of Greek quantity."[12]

with you from the brink, before
the crash—

to seize the moment . . . .
(I, ii, p. 35.)

This new freedom in stanza form (achieved without loss of rhythmic
regularity) carries over to the line. No longer do lines fall into two
halves, yet the short units in which the poem moves are regular.
Phrasal units now run from line to line, tying individual lines into
groups.

This freedom in line arrangement increases as the epic progresses
(although in some late passages Williams returns to the long line
marked by a caesura). The tendencies of Book I toward line arrangement as a reflection of content develop into sequences like this opening
scene of Book II:

Outside
outside myself
there is a world, . . .

which I approach
concretely—

The scene's the Park
upon the rock,
female to the city

—upon whose body Paterson instructs his thoughts
(concretely)

—late spring,
a Sunday afternoon!
(II, i, p. 57.)

Each group of words is a unit of measure. The paced arrangement of
the first few lines reproduces Paterson's thought in flowing rhythm;
the tercet and couplet are sharp statements with no line enjambment,
restricted both in area on the page and in expression. Williams
juxtaposed the two arrangements for contrast: approaching the world
"concretely," he found the specific scene of the tercet and couplet.
Throughout *Paterson*, the poet's thoughts tend to move either in long
measures or in short sequences connected by structure into phrases—
the interruptions of fact, in short.

Book II contains more of this "line determined by content" than other volumes. Such variety is possible because the book includes the speech of other characters as well as Paterson; each *persona* naturally has a different speech rhythm. The sermon of Klaus Ehrens, for example, has a pulsing rhythm seldom broken by pauses. Paterson's more concise comment contrasts with Ehrens' rhetoric in the following passage:

> — the spirit of our Lord that gives
> the words of even such a plain, ignorant fellow
> as I a touch of His Own blessed dignity and
> strength among you .   . . . .
>
> It was windless and hot in the sun
> where he was standing bareheaded.
>
> Great riches shall be yours!
> I wasn't born here. I was born in what we call
> over here the Old Country . . . .
>
> (II, ii, p. 83.)

In Book III Williams abandons this basis for variation as he turns almost exclusively to Paterson and his thoughts. Although the rhythms of introspection vary somewhat, these lines tend to be longer and more consistent in pattern than those provoked by the numerous speakers in Book II.

The use of longer lines to reflect thought appears also in Williams' short poems of the late forties, those of *The Clouds* and *The Pink Church*. Another dominant form is that of the "loose quatrain," basic form which Williams considered flexible, adding or subtracting lines as necessary.

> . . . Draws one stocking
> tight and
> waiting
> tilts
>
> Her hips and
> in the warm still
> air lets
> her arms
>   Fall . . .
>
> ("Philomena Andronico," *CLP*, p. 121.)

In the poems of the forties which used "free" structures, Williams seemed to be drawn to the discipline of the quatrain and tercet. The verse paragraph of "Aigeltinger," for example, is built around the tercet; of "Suzanne," around the quatrain. Fortunately, as Williams continued his search for a single form which would embody both freedom and order, his reliance on this movement by sections lessened. At the same time, a new emphasis appeared in his poetic theory.

4.

As a result of diverse experimentation, Williams realized that his basic approach was incorrect: not stanza or line but measure was the key to structure. As he wrote in 1947:

> we must break down
>   the line
>   the sentence
> to get at the unit of measure in order to build.[13]

Williams had found that order could result from a pervasive design as well as from regularity within each part of the poem. Such a design, he felt, could grow naturally from arrangements of single measures which in themselves were both flexible and regular.

To consider a foot "regular" need not imply an iambic or dactylic accent pattern, however, for if the foot were pre-conceived, only the length of line and stanza could vary; rhythms would again be inflexible. Williams concluded that the foot is not a unit of accents but one of time, and that its regularity need be only relative: "time is the real matter of measure and not stress. Elapsed time is the whole story."[14] One must be concerned not with stresses but with the "spaces in between the various stresses of the verse," spaces which are, of necessity, "variable."[15]

Measure consequently is a matter of duration. The foot may be made up as easily of one syllable and a pause as of six or seven words. Because duration is more difficult to measure than accents are to count, Williams warned that the new metric pattern required "a new sensitivity. . . . We are through with the crude 'fight' we have had to wage." Rather than battle for completely new forms, Williams conceded that "the 'new measure' is much more particular, much more related to the remote past than I, for one, believed."[16] Actually,

Williams' ideal form is very similar to the Gregorian chant: the measure remains orderly but it depends on the pace of the words, words in turn guided by the musical continuity of the whole.

It is precisely because Williams was aware that duration of time is difficult to measure that he began dividing his line into its metric units visibly. Division was necessary because the longer line had become characteristic of Williams' later work. Lines like:

> The shadow does not move. It is the water moves,
> running out. A monolith of sand on a passing barge, . . .

and:

> Today small waves are rippling, crystal clear, upon the pebbles . . .

contain several metric units, but only the poet knows the identity of each when they are written within one line.

Because Dr. Williams felt that the concept of measure was the single most important issue in contemporary poetics (largely because it had been ignored by many poets), he resolved to "make clear" his personal technique. Lines which had been written initially as:

> The most marvellous is not
> the beauty, deep as that is, but . . .

were now arranged:

> The most marvellous is not
>   the beauty, deep as that is,
>   but the classic attempt
>   at beauty . . .

Williams also used the divided line frequently throughout *Paterson* IV, of which book he wrote excitedly in 1951: "I say even that the language . . . more fits the line in the last book than in the first."[17]

Paralleling his experiments with the longer line divided into measures, Williams also utilized the by-now familiar dash and parenthesis to enforce speech rhythms.

> Rescued! new-white
>
>   (from Time's
>   dragon: neglect-tastelessness-
>   the down-beat)

                    But why?
            why the descent into ugliness that
            intervened, how
            could it have come about,
                            (the essence—...
                    ("The Old House," *CLP*, p. 116.)

A comparison of this finished poem with an earlier version from the
State University of New York at Buffalo worksheets shows that the
effects of punctuation and spacing were of great significance to
Williams:

            How beautiful the old house
            rescued and repainted, Why
            why the descent into ugliness
            that intervened, how
            could it have come about?
            Such decay, such decay of the senses
            the redundant and expensive
            the useless . . .

    In "The Desert Music," Williams' first long poem written after
his expressed desire for "clarity," he continued these techniques.
Because the narrative structure of "The Desert Music" combines
interior monologue with conversation, the rhythms and arrangements
of juxtaposed sections vary greatly. The poet reminisces in long lines
suggestive of thought, interspersed with regular short ones:

            Leaving California to return east, the fertile desert,
                    (were it to get water)
            surrounded us, a music of survival, subdued, distant, half
                            heard; we were engulfed
            by it as in the early evening, seeing the wind lift
                            and drive the sand, we
            passed Yuma . . . .

He uses both the divided line and the dramatic effects of spacing and
punctuation to re-create other phases of his thought:

                            —to tell
            what subsequently I saw and what heard

                            —to place myself (in
            my nature) beside nature

                              —to imitate
        nature (for to copy nature would be a
              shameful thing)

                          I lay myself down . . . .

In contrast, more abrupt rhythms characterize the tempo of actual speech:

        —and those two alligators in the fountain

        There were four

              I saw only two

                          They were looking
        right at you all the time   .

        Penny please! Give me penny please, mister.

                    Don't give them anything . . . .
                          (*Pictures,* pp. 110-112.)

Most of this poem is built of similar sections, rhythms dependent on content and speaker rather than on any preconception of line or structure.

Such late experiments led directly to the triadic line or *versos sueltos* structure of the mid-fifties, a structure which provided much freedom of movement within a basic regularity. In 1955 Williams termed the triadic line "my solution of the problem of modern verse . . . the culmination of all my striving after an escape from the restrictions of the verse of the past."[18] He wrote in this line from 1952 until approximately 1958:

                          . . . only the docile women
              of the party smiled at me
                    when, with my eyes
                          I accosted them.
        The nuns—but after all
              I saw only a face, a young face
                    cut off at the brows.

        It was a simple story.

                          ("The Host," *Pictures,* p. 94.)

Measure here appears regular, with each "line" divided into three units or feet. Because of the spatial arrangement, each foot has a consistent time value regardless of its actual length.

Dr. Williams advised readers to "count a single beat" for each segment of line; the resulting rhythm is "a language which we hear spoken about us every day."[19] The didactic divisions of the triadic line are especially valuable in designating a measure so familiar that one does not recognize it as measure—in a sentence such as "The nuns—but after all I saw only a face," for example.

That Williams considered these measure divisions valuable is apparent from his reading of the poems. He pauses perceptibly after most feet and at length following sentences. While his reading does not distort the content of the poem, it does emphasize the measure. The following passage is an approximation of Williams' reading of "The Descent" as recorded by Caedmon:

> The descent beckons |
>   as the ascent beckoned. ||
>   Memory is a kind
> of accomplishment, |
>   a sort of renewal |
>   even |
> an initiation, since the spaces it opens are new places |
>   inhabited by hordes |
>   heretofore unrealized . . . . |
>   (*Pictures,* p. 73.)

Pausing at the end of each foot accentuates not only the rhythms but also the grammatical completeness of each: enjambment between feet is unnecessary because structure links the three units into one line. Williams continues to use modified enjambment to connect one complete line with the next, however.

The feet in "The Descent" give the impression of being regular because the lines move steadily at a rather slow pace. Yet one foot consists of the single word *even* and another is comprised of ten words, eighteen syllables. Although the longer line slows the poem, it does not destroy the movement of the sequence as a whole. Much of this feeling of regularity may be attributed to the poem's interwoven, tapestry-like structure. The very movement of the eye provides continuity—of pace as well as content. Williams' great interest during these years in the fifteenth-century Flemish tapestry can help to explain his concept of "design"—a dominant "tone" existing despite variance within individual segments.

The chief virtue of the triadic line is that it in no way restricts the individual sentence. As Robert Lowell commented, Williams used a great variety of sentences, short phrases contrasting with rhetorical, lengthy constructions which would resemble Faulkner's if written in prose. This variety gives the poem "quick changes of tone, atmosphere, and speed."[20] Kenneth Rexroth had earlier considered the naturalness of Williams' sentences one of his poetic strengths. He titled Williams "the first American classic" primarily because "his poetic line is organically welded to American speech like muscle to bone, as the choruses of Euripides were welded to the speech of the Athenians in the market place."[21]

Although the triadic line permitted much freedom of construction, in 1955 it too was subjected to Williams' experimentation.

> The petty fury
>   that disrupts my life—
>   at the striking of a wrong key
> as if it had been
>   a woman lost
> or a fortune.   .
>   ("The Drunk and the Sailor," *Pictures*, p. 146).

Generally the poems of the 1955 *Journey to Love* have shorter units of measure, as well as dropped feet within the triadic line. Increased brevity was to be expected, however; Williams was only returning to the pace of speech which was natural for him. As he stated in 1960:

> At the present time I have been trying to approach a shorter line . . . . I wanted the shorter line, the sparer line, and yet I want to give a measured line, but the divisions of the line should be shorter . . . more terse.[22]

Nearly twenty years before he had expressed his rationale for the pace of the line: "The faster the social economic pace (the narrowing of the time dimension) of the diminishing fullness (length) of the poetic line (phrase)."[23]

Not surprisingly, experimentation within the triadic line continued in the 1958 *Paterson* V; only part of the fifth book falls into triads. Williams considered this last book an embodiment of "everything I've learned of 'the line' to date."[24] And so it is—for just as he had learned that the foot and the line are most effective when variable, he now had learned that the same is true of a total design.

> He saw buffalo
>   and more
>   a horned beast among the trees
>   in the moonlight
>   following small birds
> the chicadee . . . .

>   There is a woman in our town
>   walks rapidly, flat bellied
>   in worn slacks upon the street
>   where I saw her.
>   neither short
>   nor tall, nor old nor young
>   her
>   face would attract no
>
>   adolescent . . . .
>   (V, i, pp. 245-246; ii, p. 255.)

This modification of the triadic line was a reasonable change for Williams. Although the line provided space for the foot to vary, it was so regular in itself that it begot monotony. And just as the parts of a tapestry have their own shapes, so must the segments of the poem. The triadic line had been beautifully suited for sonorous interior monologues, but for the mélange of personal and external comments which make up *Paterson* V, it provided too little opportunity for contrast. Dr. Williams kept the variable foot, but he created richer effects with it through a variety of arrangements.

5.

SUCH new arrangement of the variable foot continues into the 1962 *Pictures from Brueghel,* where most of the poems fall into tercets and quatrains.* The need for the tapestry-like design has diminished

---

* A return to more nearly regular forms is no contradiction of Williams' theory: he had come to realize, after many years of censuring standard prosodic arrangements like the sonnet, that if the poem moves into such an arrangement naturally, that form is justified.

in these smaller segments of life; because subjects are more limited, poems are shorter. And because Williams works less frequently with presentations of his thoughts, the foot—though still variable—tends also to be shorter, as "Emily" shows. Beginning descriptively:

> your long legs
> built
> to carry high
>
> the small head
> your
> grandfather
>
> knows
> if he knows
> anything

the poem moves to subjective reference. It then continues with the child's dominant qualities: long legs give "the dance as/ your genius." The keen eyes of the knowing grandfather, however, have seen that there are obstacles to her career:

> the cleft in
> your
> chin's curl
>
> permitting
> may it
> carry you far

(Pictures, pp. 19-20.)

Because Williams shows his feeling for the child through the direct expression of detail rather than a discussion of the abstraction, love, rhythms tend to be the short phrases of objective description. The depiction is hardly simple in the sense of early Objectivist poems, but it is presented in simple language and rhythms. The shorter feet result from this intensely direct expression, as well as from the shift in point of view from reminiscence to observation.

In this final combination of musical, poetic, and visual qualities, Williams attained a form suitable for all of his poems. Using the flexible yet orderly variable foot, he could re-create his natural speech rhythms no matter what his subject. The variety of fine poems which he wrote using this metric concept is proof that his final theory of measure is valid.

Surprisingly, critics and poets alike agree on the success of the variable foot, although the only "rule" in Williams' theory is that measure be flexible. The variability which is the strength of the theory, however, also becomes its difficulty: it is impossible for other poets to use Williams' measure and line arrangements as guides to their own. In effect, each poet is thrown back to a reliance on his own ear, a reliance tempered by his recognition of a pace peculiar to each poem.

Perhaps poetry has needed this emphasis on one of the oldest poetic concepts, the poem as the voice of the poet. Because expression varies with the individual, a man can be identified through his characteristic speech. And speech as it is used in the poem can determine measure. Let measure remain variable then or—to use another of Williams' terms—*relative,* relative to each speaker-poet, to his local, and to his experience.

CHAPTER SIX

"The Song of the Fox Sparrow"

1.

I TOOK the city as my "case" to work up . . . . It called for a poetry such as I did not know, it was my duty to discover or make such a context on the "thought." To *make* a poem, fulfilling the requirements of the art, and yet new, in the sense that in the very lay of the syllables Paterson as Paterson would be discovered . . . it would be as itself, locally, and so like every other place in the world. For it is in that, that it be particular to its own idiom, that it lives.[1]

EARLIER chapters of this study have shown in part the impact of the epic *Paterson* on Dr. Williams' art. In his efforts to *"make* a poem, fulfilling the requirements of the art, and yet new," he drew all earlier successful techniques—metaphor, spatial organization, the image sequence, line and stanza determined by content—into a form which achieved the "new" for which he was searching.

Motivated by his belief that "The province of the poem is the world," Williams included as subject matter within the epic many themes which had dominated his earlier poems: man's relation to man, to woman, to nature, to the urban complex, and to art; and interrelationships within each category. He expressed this content both directly and through concrete objectification, true to his belief that "there must be a physical feature; there can't be a philosophical poem without physical features to give them character and to bring them to a head."[2]

It is primarily because Dr. Williams relied on his constant interests and his tested means of achieving their expression that *Paterson* is most accurately judged as a characteristic Williams' poem rather than as a separate entity. The epic is a progression within the poet's work, an extension of it rather than a departure from it.

Unfortunately, some critics fail to consider *Paterson* from this perspective. They demand a book-length poem of uniform excellence, the finished product of years of experimentation instead of the ground for continued invention. It is ironic that critics seem most antagonized by prosodic changes within the epic, yet prosody was admittedly one of Williams' primary concerns when he began writing *Paterson*. In 1944 he wrote that the epic "is fast becoming, as it inevitably must, a restudy of the poetic line . . . on a new sensual (auditory) basis using the local dialect as heard: counted as heard."[3]

So far as structure was concerned, one of Williams' chief goals in his halting movement toward prosodic satisfaction was "subtlety." He had written of some poems in *The Wedge,* the collection published two years before *Paterson* I, that they "abash me with their rather too obvious a putting together, more like a blob of muddy statement which should be or should have been a dandelion seed floating."[4] That Williams felt his experimentation within *Paterson* to have been successful is evident from his comment on the poem in 1954: "The construction is subtle but expressed in commonest terms. The arrangement is not common."[5]

Because most criticism of the epic focuses on structure and prosody and because Williams himself was at first deeply concerned with them, I shall in this chapter approach *Paterson* from that point of view. As Chapter IV has shown, Williams thought of poetic structure as the outgrowth of language, with various verbal devices serving as the bases for organization. The general purpose of formal structure in his poems was to create a means of expressing "the whole knowable world about me. The longer I lived in my place, among the details of my life, I realized that these isolated observations and experiences needed pulling together."[6] Such technique applies to many of Williams' short poems as well as to *Paterson* and, in part, to other contemporary epics—*The Cantos, The Wasteland,* and *The Bridge.* In essence, this pattern of organization is integral to the definition of the modern epic.

Because today's epic reflects an inordinately complex society, the subject, action, and structure of the traditional form are inadequate. As a reflection of modern man's consciousness, an identity which can no longer be represented by a simple narrative, the epic dwells on what many critics have termed "the symphonic" rather than the narrative. It is concerned with a continual present which includes both past and future. Man's consciousness provides organization as well as subject; therefore the poetic statement is a fluid, constant process. Most modern epics have in common such a sense of timelessness—or rather of the unity of all time.

Because the contemporary epic attempts to present a nearly unlimited amount of material, and because chronology is ineffectual in dealing with man's consciousness, traditional patterns of organization are unsuitable. When Randall Jarrell complains that Williams replaced drama, logic, narrative, and "sustained movement" with "mosaic techniques,"[7] he is in effect demanding just this inadequate chronological simplification. Although some readers have criticized *Paterson* for its "formlessness," others have understood the demands of the material so well that they have created terms with which to describe Williams' organization. Janet Fiscalini calls the pattern in both *Paterson* and *Yes, Mrs. Williams* "experimental generation":

> Williams' practice is to present, to pile up particulars . . . in such rhythmed arrangements that the development and reflection of motives are possible, though explicit connections, narrative or "logical," are abandoned.[8]

R. W. Flint describes the structure of *Paterson* as circling about "a set of protean, imagist-symbolist centers of force which polarize his loose, fragmentary material."[9] Albert Cook terms the structure "diffusion"; he sees it in all contemporary epics and justifies it because modern images do not cohere. In using diffusion, the poet begins with fragments which he may present, build from, or reminisce about.[10]

While each of these definitions is only partially accurate (in that none explains what does happen to achieve these general results), Williams' own statements about a "dispersive" structure show that he too was cognizant of the value in such a concept. However, his ultimate purpose was to create a unified entity, not merely to reflect the disorganization of society. Therefore, Williams' epic structure was far from "loose"; in fact, it can be considered formal. *Paterson*'s presentation is in many ways similar to that of *In the American Grain*, Williams' 1925 book which is apparently a collection of essays but actually one well-structured whole, as both Jean Garrigue and Louis Martz have emphasized. As Miss Garrigue described Williams' structural technique:

> . . . the book's *esthetique* rests in the material, in the way, that is, it is lifted out and put down against something else, in the way some

rough rude simplicity is juxtaposed against some elaborate and painted description . . . . Williams' high sense of design in maintaining this nervous balance of opposites remains a perennial pleasure . . . . Out of these parts and pieces, from documents, letters, Williams constructed, by carefully chosen data, this montage of the stream of past events that he would relate to the stream of our own unconsciousness and consciousness.[11]

The parallels between the organization of *Paterson* and that of *In the American Grain* are even more striking when one realizes that Miss Garrigue's description is of the earlier book.

Despite Williams' recognition of *dispersal* as a structural device, he emphasized consistently the counter-balancing force of *convergence*. He wrote in his preliminary definition of *Paterson* that the epic was to be "by multiplication a reduction to one." Because the aim of his epic format was unity, his techniques throughout the poem are noticeably similar.

One primary means of attaining total homogeneity even though working from disparate elements is metamorphosis. As Sister M. Bernetta Quinn has recognized, the device of a changing identity permits a comprehension otherwise impossible, particularly in characterization. For, just as in the traditional epic, the core of the modern poem is still the hero. Today's diverse milieu cannot, however, be comprehended by a simple consciousness moving toward a single goal. Therefore the hero of the twentieth-century poem must be an all-inclusive being, as Paterson is a unity of elements of man, nature, city, and art. And because many components of civilization remain mystical or mythic, the hero must identify with these aspects as well as with "realities."

In what appears to be a near-frantic effort to embody these many segments of life into one character, the contemporary poet has in most cases created a mythic-actual hero who undergoes metamorphosis within the poem, who "adopts identity after identity while yet retaining a recognizable self."[12] The heroes of Eliot and Crane exist amid changing settings in wider attempts to approximate man's difficult role in society. That Williams' protagonist acts under a variety of names—Noah, Faitoute, Dr. P., Paterson—also suggests the diverse personalities demanded by modern life.

Despite these basic similarities, however, Williams' Paterson differs from the other heroes of modern epics in that he has at least four separate identities. Few other poets have seen the natural world as a necessary character for the hero; attention has more commonly centered on man as an element of the industrial complex. Because Williams loved nature, it came to represent the beauty and stability of life in Paterson's character. The violence of nature—falls, fires, tornadoes, floods—Williams equated with man's elemental reactions. As he said of this passional quality in nature, "it gives features to the otherwise pointless force of events. It brings out characteristics of people."[13]

Yet, living as he did in the industrial east of New Jersey, with New York's skyscrapers visible across the swampland, Williams had to include the city in his concept of man: "a city is a typical thing of the modern world, it's a place where men are most operative . . . . most accomplished."[14] Williams, however, could not conceive of man as merely representative of places. The essence of the human being was too much a part of his consciousness. As he recalled, "I thought to myself: 'Well, if I am going to speak about a person, it must be an actual person, but a really heroic figure.' "[15] Therefore, he created the heroic identity of Paterson—truth-seeker, poet, doctor, lover, and completely human man. Eventually, as Williams grew older, this multiple concept merged with that of the dedicated artist, the mythic personification of art, as the poet asked:

> When you're through with sex, with ambition, what can an old man create? Art, of course, a piece of art that will go beyond him into the lives of young people, the people who haven't had time to create. The old man meets the young people and lives on.[16]

2.

BECAUSE of the diversity inherent in Williams' concept of Paterson, I earlier termed the protagonist the peak of his use of symbolic metaphor. Paterson is sometimes the city—or one area of it; again, the falls; still again, the female counterpart of the poet—and often a combination of several characters. But even when Paterson represents one identity at a time, the problem of being is not clarified: neither the falls, the woman, nor the city is a simple concept. For example, the falls as Williams depicts them represent the mystery and terror with which a superstitious people view natural wonders. They also correspond in their unbound violence with other evidences of both natural and human passion. They have identity as beauty, as comfort, and as source of death, in addition to several key metaphoric equivalents which Williams creates throughout the poem—language, thought, seminal fluid, and life force.

The poet's reliance on symbolic metaphor within *Paterson* is a pervasive technique; its use is not limited to the protagonist in his varying guises. The epic is filled with objects, people, and abstractions which are mélanges of reference evolving from nets of relationships woven throughout the five books. Even an object presented simply, objectively, in its first appearance can grow through multiple associations into an image of major significance. The dog, for example, is first presented as "just another dog/ Sniffing the trees." But in the course of the epic, the dog becomes a symbol of beauty, of the fertility lacking in the human race, of natural wisdom similar to that of trees, of selfless loyalty leading when necessary to sacrifice, and of the mythic unicorn which has its own complex of associations.

In his Preface to Book I, Williams had explained what his technique was to be for his avowed purpose of finding "beauty":

> To make a start,
> out of particulars
> and make them general, rolling
> up the sum,

(I, i, p. 11.)

With symbolic metaphor to roll up "the sum" of the many referents one image came to have within *Paterson,* Williams did progress from a concern with the particular to one with the general. Not only the meaning of the single image but that of the entire poem is broadened by this pouring interrelation of detail, the concrete particulars "rolling in/ . . . to be rained down and/ regathered into a river that flows/ and encircles."

Important as it is to literal meaning, however, symbolic metaphor is also valuable to structure. It gives the epic a more definite organization than the loosely conceived "theme-and-variation" pattern of which many critics have spoken would have done. Because of changing or ambiguous referents, the reappearance of an image often brings a new motif into *Paterson*'s fabric of meaning. Williams himself felt that the ability to include the new was of great significance: he spoke of his epic as a "fugue,"[17] a composition which he defined as having basic themes which recur at intervals, usually in the company of new elements.

Following the course of even one image throughout the epic, then, becomes increasingly difficult as its associations broaden. The reader must constantly evaluate the stated "meaning" of the image as it is presented in addition to its reciprocal flow with past meanings, its position in relation to other themes and images, and its significance in the total epic pattern (determined by frequency and weight of use as well as by the importance of the elements which it introduces). Williams' use of the mind and its thoughts throughout *Paterson* is an excellent example of his dependence on symbolic metaphor as both a verbal and a structural device.

Once Williams has presented a negative concept of most contemporary men's minds ("beds always made up"), he compares the poet's thoughts to the moving waters of the river and the falls in that they each "forever strain forward." Although the thought-falls image itself recurs, thought is also suggested whenever the falls appear alone. Even if the early formal association is not stated, the reader continues to couple the images. A few pages later, the poet sees that "the torrent in/ their minds" is inexpressible because men have "no words": "the language/ is divorced from their minds." Now the frequent images of both divorce and language are linked with the concept of mind.

The pattern grows more complicated as earlier referents join with later: when the language in itself becomes a "falls," a triangular pattern which includes thought results. The complexity of this single theme, mind, is evident in the use Williams makes of it in Book I alone. Here thought is described as a *persona* riding a bus, as a "miraculous" happening, as a "dynamo," as "trees" whose leaves are "streaming with rain," and as a "snail-like" identity which survives inclement conditions, born of "mystery" and perhaps "myth."

To these general themes of the mind as river-falls, language, the miraculous, the living, the natural, and the persistent are added those of the mind as creativity which has its culmination in an enduring art object or a relationship; the mind as invention and challenge; and the mind as the prey of decadent knowledge (books, universities, libraries). Williams' concept of mind has, in short, suffused the entire epic, reappearing as often through oblique reference and metaphoric suggestion as through direct statement in the course of the poem. In fact, once Williams sets up his many equivalents for an image, he tends to use it without specific referent.

This use of recurring images is one of the best answers to critical objections about the addition of Book V to the epic. In the seven years that elapsed between Books IV and V, many critics had judged the four books as complete. Working under the premise that Williams was using only a theme-and-variation design, critics located the major "themes" of *Paterson,* generally isolating early concepts as focal points. What many readers failed to realize was that emphasis within a "theme" could change so greatly (because of the inclusion of *new* elements in the reference pattern) that a theme in Book V might appear to be very different from the same concept as it had been presented in Book I.

The mind, for example, continues in *Paterson* V as a dominant concept, but in this last book it appears chiefly as a creative power. Williams concentrated almost exclusively on the results of that creativity, the art objects themselves. In earlier books, the stone as a chiseled form, the bottle tried by fire, and the song had been key images; but not to the extent that the Flemish tapestry is in this last book. "The Hunt of the Unicorn" provides passages of detailed description and concrete particulars which lead the poet into provocative conclusions. In the central images of the tapestry—the unicorn, the flowers, the queenly woman—Williams found objects which coupled the real with the mythic. Such unity became important because the poet, now old, saw mind as memory and dream[18] and recognized as valid a knowledge other than empirical. In fact, according to Williams, the phase of the mind which will endure is the imagination:

> through this hole
> at the bottom of the cavern
> of death, the imagination
> escapes intact
>
> •   he bears a collar round his neck
>   hid in the bristling hair.

(V, i, p. 247.)

In a later passage from Book V Williams again juxtaposed the unicorn with the mind, adding specifically the concept of a deity to the composite:

—the hunt of
        the Unicorn and
                the god of love
    of virgin birth

        The mind is the demon
        drives us   . well,
        would you prefer it to
        turn vegetable and

        wear no beard?

                                    (V, iii, p. 272.)

Such coupling had been foreshadowed by Williams' 1955 comment on
the power of the mind: "The mind's the thing . . . . I believe the mind
is the dominant force in the world today—the most valuable possession
with which to face the world."[19] It was echoed by his depiction in 1962
of "the mind the resourceful mind/ that governed the whole"[20] and by
his notation that one of his major themes for *Paterson* V was "the posi-
tive acceptance and use of knowledge."[21] Of course, the above excerpt
continues to reinforce Williams' constant association of the mind and
the body. As he had indicated vehemently in "The Clouds," "Eve,"
"To Ford Madox Ford in Heaven," and other earlier poems, man must
never forget the physical. Consequently, the mind here appears as animal and as masculine, a concept of virility rather than of pure intel-
lectuality.

    Basically, the pervasive belief in unity through multiplicity is in-
tegral to Williams' use of symbolic metaphor as well as to his specific
presentation of the mind throughout *Paterson*. As he wrote in an early
version of "Asphodel," a poem he at first considered part of *Paterson*
V: "variety coupled with singleness/ is the key . . . . A garden/ which
old men love to tend/ summarizes the mind/ with its variety."[22]

    Another example of transfer of focus within an image complex
comes in Williams' employment of woman as a necessary counterpart
to (or, at times, a part of) Paterson. Sister Bernetta's discussion of
this image as it is used in the first four books stresses the changing
identity of woman—at times depicted as a complex figure representing
society, again as the single mountain or flower. The unfertilized flower
becomes the prototype for many contemporary women: the Negro
fearing the sex act, the neurotic Cress whose letters offer slight release
for her frustration, and Phyllis and Corydon as examples of eventual

social depravity. In contrast, woman as cherished by the poet is realized to some extent in the passionate "Beautiful thing" and more completely in the figure of Madame Curie, exponent of creativity. It is interesting too that, through juxtaposition, Williams suggests that Madame Curie's creative power comes from her personal fulfillment, moving as she does "with ponderous belly."

Continuing to stress the female principle in Book V, Williams shifts his attention to the social distinction between the moral woman and the immoral, between the virgin and the whore. His concentration on woman's sexual role is only a heightened treatment of earlier themes. It is also in keeping with his use of symbolic metaphor: he employs the image metaphorically, as a step to the heretofore undiscussed topic of a deity, but he had introduced the subject as early as Book III. When the "Beautiful thing" was sexually misused, he termed her place of whoredom a "temple" and spoke of

> An insane god
> —nights in a brothel
> And if I had .
> What then?
>
> —made brothels my home?
> (Toulouse Lautrec
> again. .)
>
> (III, i, p. 134.)

The poet continues with a description of two women who, despite different cultures, "offer the same dish," the implication here similar to the question raised above, "What then?" As Williams stated in Book V (a book dedicated to Toulouse-Lautrec):

> The moral
>
> proclaimed by the whorehouse
> could not be better proclaimed
> by the virgin, a price on her head,
> her maidenhead!
> sharp practice
> to hold on to that
> cheapening it:
> Throw it away!
>
> (V, i, pp. 242-243.)

With his customary emphasis on the demands of natural emotion, Williams felt virginity irrelevant to the total consideration of "virtue." Just as he had described the whore central to "The Desert Music" in terms of mental purity ("The virgin of her mind"[23]), so he concluded that "No woman is virtuous/ who does not give herself to her lover/ —forthwith." In Williams' view of life, the coldness of a contriving virgin was like the enveloping sea from which Paterson had returned, a representation of the world's major evil—man's indifference to man.[24]

As Louis Martz has pointed out, this emphasis on the truly humane person as open and giving also dominated Williams' earlier expression of American life, *In the American Grain*. There the poet had presented Cotton Mather and other Puritans as acting with "rigid . . . inhuman clarity." In contrast, Père Rasles along with other men humble enough to feel "wonder" is the embodiment of virtue, a spirit "able to give and to receive"[25]—a spirit characterized particularly by a "sensitive mind."[26]

Through metaphoric progression, then, the female principle of the early books of *Paterson* comes finally to rest within the larger theme of virtue-art-deity dominating Book V. Williams, after years of experience, had realized that virtue is achieved only through selfless attempts to do one's best in some type of creation; and that, of all the monuments to humanity, "A WORLD OF ART" is the most lasting.

> —the virgin and the whore, which
> most endures? the world
> of the imagination most endures:
>
> Pollock's blobs of paint squeezed out
> with design!
> pure from the tube. Nothing else
> is real . .
>
> (V, i, pp. 248-249.)

A fitting conclusion to the epic is the poet's last glimpse of the Flemish tapestry, that of "a young woman . . . the virgin and the whore, an identity"—excerpted from life and "preserved," above all moral considerations, in art.

3.

As past examples have shown, Williams at times enriched his metaphoric coupling with juxtapositions which elaborated or redefined the initial image—a technique earlier termed "transitional metaphor." For example, the repeated phrase "Beautiful thing" is followed in several passages by images relating to fire ("the whole city doomed," "aflame"); in others, by images equating it with a passionate woman, a being similar to fire ("the flame's lover," "intertwined with the fire"); again, the phrase is linked through position with language, with trees, and with death. As a result of juxtaposition, the reader sees that the variable identities of the "Beautiful thing" have areas of similarity, and consequently arrives at a composite equivalent.

Not all such arrangements, however, contribute solely to meaning. At times Williams achieved needed variation in tone or rhythm through juxtaposition:

> Is it a dirty book? I'll bet
> it's a dirty book, she said.
>
> Death lies in wait,
> a kindly brother—
>
> (III, i, pp. 132-133.)

As well as being consistent with the poet's aim of achieving "a new pace, a new and unsuspected order," these variations within the epic add to the effect of "counterpoint," a term Williams used often in his late criticism. When he began writing *Paterson* in the early 1940's, he had used the word *design* as separate from *structure,* structure being the process whereby design was accomplished. In 1945 he described his means of achieving the desired design: placing spots of color on a blank wall, ignoring chronology, until full meaning was revealed at the finish. A few years later he became even more specific as he stressed the term *counterpoint.*

Williams saw the counterpointed structure as one comprising repeated independent themes, refreshed through changes in key, tone, or rhythm so that the same melody line, or the same content, could maintain interest throughout. The term was well chosen. Williams had conceived of the "overall plot and structural scheme" for *Paterson* V as being "two interchanging themes . . . in sequence but always returning." He had recognized the importance of variation within the pattern, for he spoke of using one incident which was to be "the same as in Book II *but in a different key.*"[27]

He also had realized that counterpoint is a very restrictive form, demanding a basic homogeneity in its elements as well as structural purity. Although Williams claimed that he wanted to create "amazing juxtapositions," he also knew that the reader must be able to supply the missing transitions for himself. In 1943 he criticized Louis Zukofsky for a style which made "jerky, hysterical reading" because it was "too broken, too unexplicit to bridge the gap between the writer and the reader."[28] Williams himself only rarely made the same mistake.

As Chapter V has shown, by coupling sections of diverse forms Williams often achieved striking juxtapositions without sacrificing meaning:

> Only one answer: write carelessly so that nothing that is not green will survive.
>
>> There is a drumming of submerged
>> engines, a beat of propellers.
>> The ears are water . . .
>
> (III, iii, p. 155.)

The most noticeable shift in form within *Paterson,* of course, is Williams' movement between poetry and prose. It is significant that, although the change in appearance is great, the prose sections are usually relevant to the poetry surrounding them—a prose account of a "miraculous" mink between a treatise on "invention" and the "living stone" of imagination; a description of a literal fire between accounts of the library destruction. Many juxtapositions reflect the frequent irony with which Williams viewed his world: Hamilton's plans (in prose) to create a rich industrial area are placed between excerpts from a vagrant minister's sermon cajoling his people to renounce money; the inarticulate letter from the sex-obsessed DJB follows "the emptiness of/ a cavern resounding" and precedes a "Beautiful thing" sequence. Often, too, the prose passages describe past happenings relevant to present occurrences treated in poetry. Such use of the past is consistent with Williams' belief than man must know the roots of his locale in order to live fully.

Although the thematic relation of Williams' prose to his poetry has been proved convincingly by such critics as Ralph Nash, Walter Sutton, and Louis Martz, many questions about *Paterson* still center on

Williams' use of prose as a *form*. One explanation is the poet's, that he felt a basic identity between poetry and prose: "life . . . isn't any more poetry than prose."[29] The prose gives "a metrical meaning to or emphasizes a metrical continuity between all word use . . . . prose and verse are both *writing*."[30] That Williams felt the two to be somewhat parallel is evident also in his emphasis on what he called a "prose construction" for poetry—the use of direct statement, normal syntax, and colloquial vocabulary. There is a striking similarity as well between Williams' criticism of poetry and prose. In both cases, he stressed conciseness, reticence, factual expression, and organization dependent on techniques of juxtaposition rather than transition.

Yet with his acute ear for rhythms, Williams also recognized the essential rhythmic differences between the two forms, and utilized the contrast their juxtaposition provided. As he wrote in 1941,

> the verse itself is something of great interest to me. I've been tearing my head apart for years to get at a mode of modern verse suitable for a long poem which would be as simple as speech itself and subtle as the subtlest brain could desire on the basis of measure.[31]

Dr. Williams unquestionably succeeded in finding interesting rhythms; *Paterson* is filled with a variety of measures—in prose passages as well as in poetry, for Williams approached the prose technique with his usual inventiveness.

Some passages, especially those relating to historic events long past, are literal repetitions of the original account, a practice Williams had utilized in some chapters of *In the American Grain*. The poet felt that the characteristic speech of the period provided valuable insight into both the culture and the speaker presented. Other passages were written by Williams but in a manner reminiscent of the original style, changed to achieve clarity. Many factual descriptions are as simple and direct as good journalistic accounts; these objective statements often appear amid highly emotional poetic passages, serving simultaneously to bring the reader back to "the thing" itself and to slow the poem.

In other passages, chiefly those taken from either real or imaginary letters, words and rhythms characterize the writers. The distraught Cress is immediately recognizable from any excerpt, as is the socially-oriented poet whose concerns lie everywhere but with the poem. Letters from minor figures—Josie, DJB, Edward, A. G., and T.—add variety to tempo, just as do the words of various speakers within the poetry of the epic.

The letters convey material valuable both for thematic development and for characterization and have an important relation to one of the epic's central themes, that of the need for a satisfactory language. Just as meaningless sounds rush incomprehensibly among men, so are Cress's letters intended to move in a "tumbling stream . . . impersonating the falls." In his unpublished notes for *Paterson*, Williams described the effect he desired:

> Run it simultaneously with the poem:
> all through . . .
>
> in BLOCKS without paragraphing:
>
> it is the FALLS, continually falling:
> use it as background to everything
> else, to heighten everything else and
> to stitch together every other thing.

Of the relation between poetry and prose, Williams wrote that every section of poetry was to be "worked up" and "finished as well as possible."

> BUT—juxtaposed to them are unfinished pieces—put in without fuss—for their very immediacy of expression—as they have been written under stress, under LACK of a satisfactory form
>
> —or for their need to be just there, the information.[32]

True to his plan, Williams used some prose which conveyed information and other passages which expressed emotion, the latter convincing the reader of the ineffectiveness of language through actual incoherence. It is significant that Williams' early drafts of *Paterson* include the original letters from which segments were excerpted, the letters divided into sections by the poet's pencil for the typist to incorporate as "blocks."

The progression in the kind of prose used within the various books of the epic is also important. Amid a few personal letters, excerpts from history dominate Book I, a history easily identifiable as Paterson's. All accounts are similar in that they describe "miraculous" happenings. Just as does the poetry of this book, Williams' prose focuses attention on Paterson as a recognizable place, in both its early and its present history filled with an elemental character of superstition and mystery.

Book II is dominated by Cress's emotional letters, reflecting chiefly her isolation and poverty—of both money and affection; and by accounts of historic happenings directly related to the plight of man (and Cress) in contemporary society. The latter refer primarily to Hamilton's ambitious plans for creating an industrial giant from Paterson, plans made with no mention of the kind of lives people in that area would have as a result. Other sections of prose emphasize the *present* state of man—his sterility and indifference—written as they are in the present idiom.

Although Cress's letters do not continue into Book III, prose excerpts from history (now a mixture of recent happenings and early) re-emphasize man's inhumanity. Passages in Part I of this book deal with blatant evil; those in Parts II and III with sacrifice, an early but now unfamiliar means of atonement. These prose accounts lead to the description of the artesian well which exists in Paterson despite what Williams describes as "muck," "detritus," "a pustular scum," "decay," and "choking lifelessness."

Williams carries his depiction of man's cruelty even further in Book IV as historical passages relate to senseless murders. Other prose sections, in contrast, reflect the poet's personal life—poetry, medicine, nature, discovery. This separation between subjective reference and the realization of man's darkest evil foreshadows the motifs to come in Book V, all increasingly personal and increasingly isolated from social conditions.

Of the many prose segments in Book V, not one refers specifically to Paterson as a locale. Considering that Williams' subtitle for the epic had originally been "Any/Every Place," his move to a more generalized locality is not surprising; he had declared early in *Paterson* V, "Anywhere is everywhere." Just as in the poetry of this last book, Williams in prose moved into the worlds of memory and art. His memories are necessarily personal, focusing chiefly on kinds of fulfillment—sexual, humane, professional, and artistic. It is significant also that the only prose segment here which could be considered "historical" is taken from the Bible.

These thematic parallels between the prose passages of the five books of *Paterson* and those of its poetry I see as further proof that the epic is truly a unified whole.

4.

VIEWING *Paterson* as a design in counterpointed and thus related elements—a design relying for much of its coherence on symbolic and transitional metaphors—the reader is impressed with the integral role of theme to structure. When the epic is considered (as it sometimes is) a sporadic collection of the poet's observations made walking through his world, nearly half the content of the poem seems irrelevant— mythic references, episodes from history, inclusions from another's consciousness. Although such organization may be suggested in places, Williams initially took specific care to explain that Paterson is asleep, "the thunder/ of the water filling his dreams! Eternally asleep, his dreams walk about." As a dreaming giant, Paterson is consequently never limited to thoughts prompted by mere external observation. Having emphasized in Book I the "wonder" in life, Williams describes his interest throughout the epic as being in "the imagination, the dream . . . final result, the miracle."[33] The reader can therefore expect far more than a simple chronological narrative.

Williams considered *Paterson* his full statement of life. For that reason he added Book V to the first four, even while knowing that it would provoke critical dissension. In fact, Williams' worksheets have recently disclosed that he was working on a sixth book even after the 1958 publication of *Paterson* V. Having waited more than twenty years before attempting to write the epic, he naturally expected it to encompass all of his knowledge and his technique. *Paterson* fulfills this expectation by conveying his ideas through a variety of devices. For example, both Williams' blending of excerpts from the past and present and his organizational pattern indicate that he saw chronology as an inadequate presentation of Time. More effective than either of these devices in emphasizing his sense of timelessness are the images of the rolling snake, the serpent with its tail in its mouth, the nine wives all "growing" from a single log of experience, and the river which returns to its beginnings.

Ridding himself of the artificial distinction between categories of time, Williams also replaced what he felt were equally artificial social distinctions (between the virgin and the whore, the leading citizen and the pauper) with personal criteria for "goodness." Compelled by his sense of honesty to present a damning picture of some contemporary men, he alleviated his censure by including images of the kind, the passionate, the sympathetic—those willing to sacrifice themselves for others. As his depiction of the supposedly corrupt Phyllis showed (he referred to her as "lovable" despite his intent in creating her), Williams felt that the human situation was reparable: "My civilization is not ramshackle to me at all it is merely beshitted. . . . [Men must] learn to tolerate each other, to be generous minded toward each other."[34] His 1950 definition of the poet showed that Williams felt him to be a man who "believes in his world, he believes in his people, and that's the reason he's a poet . . . basic faith in the world."[35]

Not surprising, then, is the poet's pitiful cry of "divorce" as he sees men isolated from society, each other, women, creation, and consequently life. Neither is it surprising that one of the central themes of *Paterson* is the poet's search for a means of union. The most obvious solution to a man of Williams' occupation was language, but he found that meaningless words have too often replaced the articulate speech necessary for communication. The printed word is even less effective. Therefore Williams turned to physical relationships and, finally, to a poetry which borrowed much from graphic art as his means of expression.

It should perhaps be stated that *Paterson* is not primarily concerned with language, as many critics have stated; it is rather a study of man's search for relationships with other people. Language is a technique, not an end in itself. For this reason Williams could turn almost exclusively to graphic art, as he did in Book V, without violating the thematic unity of *Paterson* as a whole.

This turn to art as a "virtuous" means of communication resolved another of the dichotomies running throughout the epic—the distinction made between the real and the mythic. Because the imagination in Williams' ethic of life is a primary source of existence, the artist (or any man truly alive) cannot divorce himself from the imaginative world; in fact, if the conditions of real society stifle his activity, he may turn increasingly to that world. But such distinction is inaccurate: to Williams there was none. Throughout the early books of *Paterson,* he built from accounts of actual happenings considered "miraculous" by the people. Using these nuclei of wonder, he moved easily between factual and imaginative worlds, elements of one suffusing the other.

In Book V, for example, the unicorn, the fields of flowers, and the queenly woman dominate the poem. The images come directly from the tapestry, but they are used with more than factual significance. The poet in the course of the book equates the unicorn with martyrdom, the female principle, death, an artist, and himself. The poet in particular shares with the beast perseverance, selflessness, compatibility with nature, and devotion to imaginative living, as shown by this last portrait of Paterson, "the King-self" who had gone on

> living and writing
>   answering
> letters
>   and tending his flower
> garden, cutting his grass and trying
> to get the young
>   to foreshorten
> their errors in the use of words which
> he had found so difficult, ...
>
>   Though he is approaching
> death he is possessed by many poems.
>   (V, iii, pp. 268-269.)

One can hardly bring the words of myth and reality into closer harmony.

Paterson for all its complexity of structure and its evidence of technical skill is most memorable finally for this expression of unmistakably genuine conviction. It lives as testimony of Williams' definition of art as "a re-embodiment of feeling, of sanctity, of devotion to the human freight that the artist . . . must bear."[36] Art must be "something related in a concentrated form with the basic interests of man's life."[37]

In *Paterson,* Williams' convictions about these "basic interests" are inescapable: like woman, man must use his strength to endure— even in the midst of perversion, he must follow his intimate concepts of virtue; even if collared and tethered, he must be free through his imagination; even if but a man, he must identify so selflessly with the people and objects of his local culture that he becomes as rich a character as Paterson:

> a local pride; spring, summer, fall and the sea; a confession; a basket; a column; a reply to Greek and Latin with the bare hands; a gathering up; a celebration; . . . a taking up of slack; a dispersal and a metamorphosis.

CHAPTER SEVEN

"It Has Been Accomplished"

1.

IN 1954 Kenneth Rexroth saw *The Desert Music* as the beginning of a new era of accomplishment for Williams, then nearing seventy:

> From now on, as Williams grows older, he will rise as far above his contemporaries as Yeats did above his in his latter years. The fruit has ripened on the tree.[1]

Rexroth found these poems excellent both in technique and in expression of Williams' basic concepts. The poet's empathetic concern with man which dominated *Paterson* and many of his earlier poems also permeates *The Desert Music* and the books to follow, the 1955 *Journey to Love* and the 1962 Pulitzer Prize winning *Pictures from Brueghel*. That Williams came to write his finest poems at such an advanced age proves the truth of his statements about art and life, that success "comes often of a lifetime's efforts"[2] and that the artist "has to live and . . . live long *in* his world."[3]

Williams' achievement in these late poems is most assuredly the result of a "lifetime's efforts." In technique as well as in theme the poet progressed logically, using the results of earlier experiments and the motifs of earlier subjects in this final blending of technical skill and human concern.

Most reactions to these late poems, however, were dependent not on Williams' themes but rather on his technical innovation. Critical response centered largely on "the variable foot" and the tapestry-like triadic line. Although these devices appeared to be new, Williams had used the variable foot—though not so named or so arranged—for at least a decade. In fact, a study of his last poems shows that Williams was continuing to work for the same effects which had dominated his earlier poetry. To achieve his ideal poem, he depended on the principles of interrelation (to create the complex whole), concentration (to insure "instantaneous" impression), and indirection (to avoid sentimentality). These three technical principles were as constant in Williams' poetics as was his concern with the local and its speech.

It is true, however, that an emphasis on only one of these principles would cause technical variation within a group of poems. In the early fifties, Williams was deeply concerned with clarity and completeness of statement. In 1951 he wrote that he had to "make clear" his concepts of life, that he had to present "a full statement."[4] This conviction strengthened his emphasis on interrelation, often at the expense of concentration and indirection. Therefore, while the poems of *The Desert Music* and *Journey to Love* could never be labeled didactic, they do contain more direct statement than most of Williams' poems. His masterful long poem of this period, "Asphodel, That Greeny Flower," shows clearly his use of devices necessary to interrelation.

The triadic line itself, of course, provides both thematic and rhythmic interrelation as lines enjamb and motifs recur. The very movement of the eye insures continuity: all units and lines are part of a flowing pattern which ends only with the poem's conclusion:

> It is winter
>> and there
>>> waiting for you to care for them
> are your plants.
>> Poor things! you say
>>> as you compassionately
> pour at their roots
>> the reviving water.
>>> Lean-cheeked . . .
>>>> (*Pictures*, p. 175.)

While the individual units of the triadic line do not necessarily enjamb (their staggered position providing automatic visual continuity), the last foot of each line often does run on to maintain the consistent pace. Here also the definite pauses—periods and exclamation points—occur within the first two units so that the pace of the total line is not broken, except intentionally. The last foot quoted, "Lean-cheeked," moves on to "I say to myself" and consequently provides more than rhythmic progression as Williams shifts unobtrusively from a descriptive section to one of introspection. In this manner thematic relation as well as smooth progression between kinds of expression is achieved.

Aside from the triadic line itself, Williams' most striking means of achieving interrelation is the symbolic metaphor of the flower. The poet provides many referents for the image, which is also used literally: it is a source of pleasure, man without cupidity, the good wife, fact, the poem, the poet's gift, and the work of the imagination. One image thus embodies nearly everything good in the poem, or as Williams writes, "Are facts not flowers/and flowers facts/or poems flowers/or all works of the imagination,/interchangeable?"

Non-symbolistic images also serve to interrelate, especially in descriptive sections. Williams presents the poet's wife being given "steps" in order to "mount/again to think well/of me." With no transition, the poet immediately after this statement describes "the statue/of Colleoni's horse." This description is followed by that of another horse "rampant/roused by the mare," and both conclude in the personification of a "fast freight" which "thundered through/ kicking up the dust." Four images relating to one central theme consequently have joined quite disparate subjects.

Because Williams discusses many subjects within "Asphodel," the poem's structure must permit easy inclusion. His solution is an organization which represents man's thought in all its diversity, complexity, and apparent disorder. The poem moves rapidly from one subject to another, blending elements into a unified statement. For example, Williams moves from a consideration of his own pride to discuss "heads." By leaving the latter undefined, he can comment on both flowers and men. The sequence ends with a metaphor equating flowers and human nobility: "the heads of most men I see/ . . . are full of cupidity./Let us breed/from those others. They are the flowers of the race." In only fifteen lines, the subject has been changed and broadened through a reasonable progression of association.

So that the poem can represent the movement of a consciousness, it must include much first-person comment, as this does. The experiences used as illustrations also come from the poet's life—"the heads of most men I see at meetings"—or from his memories—"the fields which we knew as children." That these concrete experiences are juxtaposed with many comments of direct address to "you," the poet's wife, also creates the impression of immediacy.

Another means of unifying the subject matter of the poem is the type of theme-and-variation structure Williams had perfected in *Paterson,* with motifs recurring at intervals. For example, early in Part III of "Asphodel," the wife is moved by kindness to revive her flowers and forgive the poet. Twenty lines later Williams again refers to her act, "You have forgiven me/making me new again." Part III has begun with the related question, "What power has love but forgiveness?"—a question later repeated in the poet's declaration that he has come to her "to be forgiven." The theme of forgiveness is basic to the entire poem as well.

"Asphodel" is unified too by its total design. There are few formal transitions; indeed, as presentation of thought the poem gains much reality from the omission of explicit connectives. Instead Williams uses juxtaposition, allusion, and ambiguity:

> Sweet, creep into my arms!
> I spoke hurriedly
> in the spell
> of some wry impulse
> when I boasted
> that there was
> any pride left in me . . .

The natural tendency is to read the second line, "I spoke hurriedly," in conjunction with the first. The second is, however, the beginning of a section of reminiscence which refers to an earlier passage of the poem. In the process of following the ambiguously placed line, the reader finds himself in a new context.

"Asphodel" offers many such examples of effective interrelation of parts. It also shows that emphasis on interrelation limits the concentration to be attained. If explanations are to be clear, statements must be complete; if illustrations are to be adequate, several examples are necessary. Here, rather than suggesting one side of a comparison, Williams presents both sides in full: "Having your love/I was rich. Thinking to have lost it/I am tortured/and cannot rest." Frequently the poet provides careful transition, purposely avoiding the montage effect he once would have sought:

> He wore a beard
> parted in the middle,
> a black beard,

```
and a hat,
        a brown felt hat
            lighter than
  his skin. His eyes,
        which were intelligent,
            were wide open . . .
```

This explicit description continues for fifteen lines, Williams identifying each object and associating it with the *persona: "His* brown socks/ were about *his* ankles./ In *his* breast pocket/ *he* carried . . ."

Line structure also makes condensation difficult: three units are necessary to complete each line. Although rhythms within individual feet vary, the regular arrangement of the line cannot help but restrict any tendency to condense.

Although intensification is hampered in some ways, Williams does achieve it in many places. For example, "Lean-cheeked" is used alone to describe the poet deprived of love. The abrupt statements of the poet as *persona* sharpen the poem's total pace: "Do not believe it," "Their women had big buttocks," "It will cure us both." Conversation used within the poem is also concise and direct. Because the poet's thought moves slowly, these shorter sentences add needed contrast.

Most of the effects of concentration parallel those of indirection, Williams' normal tendency of presenting rather than commenting. Even his emphasis on complete clarity cannot hide his propensity toward suggestion. He tempers a necessary baldness of expression with symbolic metaphor; although sentences are phrased bluntly, they center on undefined images. By using devices appropriate to the representation of thought, Williams also achieves presentation; the reader must follow the structure of the poem closely in order to apprehend its complete meaning. Consequently, despite an acknowledged emphasis on interrelation, this poem and the others of the mid-fifties show that Williams never forgot that his basic technical aim was three-fold.

2.

ONE structural change necessitated by Williams' desire to treat a subject fully was the increased length of the poem. As he had realized when he began writing *Paterson,* the longer a poem is the more carefully it must be structured. Williams' new attention to organization is as evident in these last poems as it was in his epic.

One of the most interesting of these late structural patterns is the symphonic. Many poems within *The Desert Music* are divided into four sections corresponding generally to those of a symphony. The first section introduces all themes of the poem; the second is a slower-moving section of development; the third, contrastingly rapid in pace, contains further development; and the fourth once again fully relates all themes, this time on a more impressive scale. Both "To Daphne and Virginia" and "Asphodel" end with a recapitulatory short section, a type of coda. In others, Williams gives sections appropriate musical designations: "The Clouds," for example, contains a third division justly entitled "Scherzo."

"The Orchestra" provides clear illustration of this symphonic arrangement carried over into the theme of the poem as well—poetic technique described in musical terms, leading ultimately to the issue of man's relation to man. One dominant theme is that of the necessity for wholeness; not "a flute note" but rather "the relation/ of a flute note/ to a drum" is the desired effect of any composition. The task of presenting "the whole" is difficult, however, because man is "half-reluctant" to listen; therefore Williams advises "Repeat/ and repeat the theme/ and all it develops." The coda implies that natural means are inadequate to attain an "assembled order":

> The birds twitter now anew
> but a design
> surmounts their twittering.
> It is a design of a man
> that makes them twitter.
> It is a design.
> (*Pictures*, p. 82.)

The bird in these closing lines echoes the opening metaphor, the orchestra seen as "a cacophony of bird calls" powerful enough to lift the sun. Moving by means of transitional metaphor, Williams relates the sun to mankind which struggles "unattuned" to find "a common tone." The resolution of Part I comes in the metaphor equating love, music, and the sun:

> Love is that common tone
> shall raise his fiery head
> and sound his note.

Following this moderately fast pace, the lento or adagio movement begins with a discussion of the purpose of an orchestra-poem. It concludes with a very slow description:

But the ear
in a half-reluctant mood
stretches
. . and yawns.

The ritard which leads to the ending is achieved through open vowel sounds (*to, these, sounds, wrong, note, wholly, flute*), the short feet of *stretches* and *and yawns,* and the pause which opens the third foot, emphasized by the spaced periods. That the interval after the adagio section is much wider than that before it also indicates a slowness consonant with the pace of the ending.

The third section, also devoted to thematic development, is characteristically allegro, used to "enliven the scene" just as the violins are, "pizzicato." "As the pace mounts" in this movement, the poem builds into the climactic fourth, where all themes reappear more fully related. Even such a detail as the French horn has thematic importance. Horns, like the woodwinds in the opening passage, are often used to suggest nature and the outdoors; with the horns professing love, all three themes are again united. They are further restated in the "coda" already described.

Since poetry is, after all, a verbal art, its tie with music should not be forced. The rhythms and subject matter of each section in "The Orchestra" do, however, make such a structural parallel plausible. Williams was admittedly thinking in terms of music during the forties and fifties. As he reads the poem on record, variations in tempo by section are obvious. The large musical rhythms of the poem can be heard clearly, especially when the poet as *persona* bursts into the poem with his contrasting prose instructions:

Say to them:
"Man has survived hitherto because he was too ignorant to know how to realize his wishes. Now that he can realize them, he must either change them or perish."

These longer lines move rapidly (or so Williams reads them), providing contrast perhaps as intentional as that of the symphonic cymbal crash.

Although not all poems of *The Desert Music* follow this arrangement, many begin or end with sections of thematic presentation and include sections which develop one of the primary motifs more fully. The structures of "The Descent," "To Eleanor and Bill Monahan," "To a Dog Injured in the Street," "The Yellow Flower," "The Mental Hospital Garden," and "The Host" can be designated generally as symphonic.

With characteristic invention, Williams arranged most of the poems in his next book, the 1955 *Journey to Love,* in simpler, single-unit structures. A return to description as his principal subject made sections of thematic development unnecessary. "The King," "A Negro Woman," "To a Man Dying on His Feet," "Address:," "The Drunk and the Sailor," and "A Smiling Dane" begin or end with subjective comment, but each poem is intended chiefly to present an object or a scene in vivid detail, not to dwell on the poet's introspection about an object.

With the poems of *Journey to Love,* Williams was in fact returning to more characteristic techniques. He liked the short, quick-moving line; the poem which presented its content rather than telling it; the abstraction seen in terms of actual objects or persons instead of as bald words; the art object stripped to essential detail so that its impression is made quickly. The poems of the triadic line, although personally necessary to Williams in one period of his life, were incompatible with many of these pervasive artistic beliefs.

As some of his last poems show, only a short poem limited to a single subject could satisfy all his poetic demands. Subjects, however, could not be the static depictions of Objectivism, isolated from all context. They had to re-create a complete area of life; they had to present the "complex" as "simple."*

Considered musically, Williams' ideal poems must be most like the song in their fusion of melody based on speech inflections with a human voice in deeply personal expression. They must blend the multiple components of a subject into a tightly unified whole, expressed succinctly, subtly, and personally.

3.

THE resulting poems are those of *Pictures from Brueghel.* The 1962 collection contains a central body of work consistent in structure, rhythm, tone, and economy—surrounded by a periphery of poems showing Williams' tireless experimentation. The central poems, represented here by "Elaine," deal in apparent simplicity with the poet's reaction to one image of life:

---

* As the poet-playwirght Hubert explained in *Many Loves:* "if it's to be new, it must be complex. . . . But some one/ must first have seen the complex/ simple, simple as water flowing . . ./ so that it appears an easy matter."[5] Statements throughout Williams' late poems also emphasize the basic simplicity of the subject presented: the sparrow makes a "simple statement" as does the dictionary concerning Nell Gwyn; the story of the nun is "simple," as is that of the Christ: "a simple story./ Love is in season."

poised for the leap she
is not yet ready for
—save in her eyes

her bare toes
starting over the clipt
lawn where she may

not go emphasize summer
and the curl
of her blonde hair

the tentative smile
for the adult plans laid
to trap her

calves beginning to flex
wrists
set for the getaway

(*Pictures*, p. 18.)

Related thematically to many of Williams' late poems in that it deals with love, "Elaine" presents the emotion rather than describing it. Williams' careful attention to detail shows his feeling for the child because "you can't write about something unimportant to yourself."[6] This belief of the poet's is the theme of another of his late poems, "The Painting," in which he describes a "beautifully drawn" portrait of a child as a "defeat" because the artist was indifferent to her subject.

Of the many modifications in technique between the poems of the triadic line and "Elaine," most important to all considerations of the poem is Williams' return to rendering from comment. By presenting his subject instead of explaining it, the poet avoids excessive verbalization: no longer an abstraction requiring definition and illustration, the subject is the very concrete itself.

Presentation alone, however, does not assure interrelation. The subject in itself must relate several components into a whole. In the central image of Elaine, for example, Williams presents the timeless conflict of youth and age, eagerness and caution, complete with the child's feeling of repression in the word "getaway." Determination evident in her eyes, the conspiracy ("plans laid to trap her") forces the child to be cunning. She begins slowly, only her toes moving; her smile is "tentative," awaiting reaction to her disobedience.

Because of its compact detail, the poem can also include the time and scene, as well as both an objective physical description of the child and a subjective coupling of her with summer. While the poem reflects truthfully Elaine and her action, it also contains an entire complex of feelings—those of the child, the poet, and (by implication) the other adults. Yet response to the poem is immediate because of its concentration.

This instantaneous impression of a whole depends primarily on structure. The poem itself is a single sentence, with "toes emphasize" serving as the core for early clauses and the concluding descriptive series. Because lines are left open, the eye sweeps through the entire poem. To achieve continuity, Williams has placed what punctuation is used at the beginning of lines rather than at the ends. Early lines, those more directly involved in the child's action, enjamb to set the poem and the child in motion.

Although Williams continues to use the variable foot, his present tercet arrangement increases tempo and suggests the definite outline of a form. As Chapter IV has pointed out, these poems arranged in a structure limited to one area on the page resemble a painting, just as those following the triadic line organization resemble a tapestry. The artist has his choice of a wide view of life in which many separate scenes are interwoven or of one limited area presented in depth. Each technique has its advantages—and its disadvantages.

One advantage of the single view is that its brevity creates the impression of wholeness. In such condensation, each word becomes important. As in "Elaine," any peripheral detail is conveyed through a single word or phrase which is also relevant to the central image presented. Her "tentative" smile, for example, suggests the child's feelings as well as the reasons for those feelings, yet it is ostensibly a detail of visual description.

Another advantage is that the reader will more easily follow the single view than the broad perspective, and will accordingly need only indirect help from the poet. This statement does not imply, however, that the poet withdraws from the poem as he was to do during Objectivism. Like the song, these poems are primarily expressions of the poet's feelings; the element of objective description is secondary. Williams' comments about the portrait as an art form—to which these late poems have been compared in Chapter IV—also emphasize the role of the artist's personal response in such creation. Williams believed that the portrait artist finds "a new object—his own imaginary image in the terms of the subject before him. Himself—in all its multiple implications . . . . The artist is always and forever painting only one thing: a self portrait."[7]

The most apparent disadvantage of the poem of more limited scope is that it cannot include as many points of view or peripheral details as the tapestry. As "Elaine" illustrates, however, brief economically worded poems can include many details of the subject presented. In fact, by their very limitation these poems often penetrate to an essential area of life. As Denise Levertov wrote of them in a letter to Williams:

> In your "small" poems, by which I mean simply short poems that apparently focus on some single detail, there is always the reverberation of the total; not of any academic symbolism but of your vision of the world, or of what it is to be living; so that every poem is at once a complete *thing* . . . and at the same time relates to all your other poems.[8]

Many of Williams' late poems deal with the same general subject; because each treats one well-defined image, however, thematic families may not be evident. The danger is, of course, that one poem of an entire subject complex may be mistaken for the poet's total comment. For example, Williams sometimes views growing old with optimism; sometimes, with bitterness. The "tragic winter thoughts" of "The Woodthrush" parallel the tone of "Song," in which beauty is described as "no more than a sop/ when our time/ is spent and infirmities/ bring us to/ eat out of the same bowl." Contrastingly, the tranquil acceptance of old age dominates "To a Woodpecker" and "The Snow Begins," as the formerly murderous snow becomes "gay curtains." A related series of poems presents a kind of immortality in the timelessness of art and the imagination. Art objects live after artists have died, memories assume shapes of reality: "In old age they walk in the old man's dreams and still walk/ in his dreams, peacefully continuing in his verse/ forever."[9]

Williams' worksheets again provide valuable insight into his poetic aims during this last decade. In its final form the poem "Paul" describes a boy's satisfaction as he catches, cleans, and eats the black-fish. One section also suggests the deeper issue of each man's need for his own language: "seize that glistening/ body translated/ to/ that language you/ will understand." In early versions, however, this brief comment was only one of many philosophical instructions from grandfather to grandson:

> You have nothing
>
> more to learn from
> life because
> after all starting from

deep within the matrix
you
will see everything

on the fish's way
up to the surface . . .

There are unexpected overtones in Williams' early descriptions of the fish: "He struggles manfully . . . ./ as he (or she) feels/ his world, the water/ slipping/ away from him"; and in the personal inference gained from that struggle:

give me a fulcrum
and
I can move

the earth, we start
in the water.[10]

These early versions show clearly that Williams himself thought his "small" late poems unquestionably concerned with man's total world.

As in his earlier work, Dr. Williams here relied often on figurative language to increase the suggestivity—and consequently the inclusion—of the poem. "Portrait of a Woman at Her Bath" is one of the most effective of these late poems built around figures of speech:

it is a satisfaction
a joy
to have one of those
in the house

when she takes a bath
she unclothes
herself she is no
Venus

I laugh at her
an Inca
shivering at the well
the sun is

glad of a fellow to
marvel at
the birds and the flowers
look in

(*Pictures*, p. 46.)

Consistent with his definition of the portrait as art form, Williams here presents a thoroughly subjective view of the woman. His statement is both direct—"it is a satisfaction," "I laugh at her"—and metaphoric. Because of Williams' ethic of the harmony between nature and natural man, the figures of speech—the Inca metaphor as well as the responses of the sun, birds, and flowers—are highly complimentary. His praise is only heightened through the context of pretended indifference to "one of those" and "a woman."

Early versions of the poem show the centrality of the Inca figure. Williams' progression after "she is no/ Venus" is as follows:

Draft 1   but in
           the New World she rouses
           the sun
           is brighter

Draft 2   but when she rouses
           she shows herself
           to be
           something from a New World

At first the woman's presence creates a "New World"; then, with his usual realism, Williams places her in a more mundane context but sees her as a representative of another world. In the next variation, he considers her "something of/ an allied god from the New World." Apparently dissatisfied with the vagueness of "an allied god" and hoping to make the tie with America stronger, he next tries "Aztec" before finally arriving at "Inca naked at the well/ seeing her shiver/ I laugh at her." The final version deletes the redundant "naked" (she is already "unclothed") and ends

          an Inca
          shivering at the well

                                        (Yale Collection).

4.

"PORTRAIT of a Woman at Her Bath" is also characteristic of Williams' late poems in its subject matter. Here the poet has focused his attention on a person whom he loves, acting within the confines of a local now limited to home and neighborhood—the garden, a neighbor's house, the street outside. As Williams grew old, weakened by the series of heart attacks and strokes that caused his death, the boundaries of his physical world became very narrow indeed.

As if to compensate, he turned at times to the realms of imagination and memory. Writing in 1955 that "Memory/ is liver than sight,"
he affirmed in "The Descent," a poem that was one of his favorites:

> Memory is a kind
> of accomplishment,
> a sort of renewal
> even
> an initiation, since the spaces it opens are new places
> inhabited by hordes
> heretofore unrealized,
> of new kinds— ...
>
> (*Pictures*, p. 73.)

It is true that Williams' reminiscences provide subject matter for
many of his late poems—those concerned with spring flowers, children
in the cemetery, the production of his play *Many Loves*, his illnesses.
However, more of the poems continue to deal with his immediate
concerns; even at seventy-nine Williams was not ready to relinquish
his contemporary local. He wrote of his grandchildren, his wife, art
still pleasing to him (Sappho, tapestries, Brueghel's paintings), Russia
and Gagarin's space flight, mail that he received. Two of his last poems
published deal with very current subjects—one with Stormy, the
Williams' young Shetland sheep dog; the other, "Cézanne," with one
of his late poetic theories, including references to a recent book of
Allen Ginsberg's.

There were, of course, decided changes within Williams' familiar
images—he wrote of winter rather than spring, of "December birds"
and fields of snow instead of flowers. As Chapter II has stated, however, the poet's basic philosophy had not changed. It had only been
strengthened. Love still rules the world because some men know that it
must and are willing to live accordingly, with virtue. Williams continued to believe in self-determinism; no matter what a man's cir-
cumstances, he can find fulfillment in human relationships, nature, art,
and dedication, providing he approaches life with humility. Nothing
satisfying, however, is easy. Man must set a goal for himself com-
parable to that of the sparrow whose song reawakened the world of
Paterson. And of all goals, the most valuable is that of an expression
in which man uses his mind.

Persevering, loving, dedicated, perceptive—Williams' ideal man is
also an aging man, experienced in the affairs of the world and in his
ability to meet them. As he wrote in an early version of "Asphodel":

> . . . a young man
> is all false starts.
> He does not finish
> anything. He has
> no center from which to start.
> (Yale Collection.)

Perhaps this is the most indelible impression of these last poems: that William Carlos Williams had found a "center," a spiritual and philosophical identity which enabled him to maintain his earliest optimistic beliefs and even to expand them: "Death is not the end of it . . ."

> If a man die
> it is because death
> has first
> possessed his imagination.

5.

THE thematic unity of all Williams' work—prose and poetry, fiction and criticism—testifies to his central philosophy just as his continuous technical progress proves his belief that craft is essential to art. Consistency in both respects was important to Williams. He stated about his use of recurring themes, "All I have ever written is one writing. After the introduction everything else linked."[11] Theme became increasingly significant to Williams as he resolved his technical problems. As he wrote in 1941:

> Perhaps some of us lay too much stress on the value of literature as excellence in itself. You got to have a message, a MESSAGE! . . . You got to have something to say . . . that's the secret of the thing.[12]

Technique, however, never lost its importance for Williams. His criticism of Carl Sandburg's late work shows again his conviction that technical direction is necessary to even the most gifted artist.

> Search as we will these poems have technically no motivating spirit that is held in the front of the mind to control them. Without a theory, as Pasteur once said, to unify them a man's observations degenerate into random and repetitious gestures.[13]

Emphatic as he was about both theme and theory, Williams did not ignore the intuitive stages of creation. As he explained the poetic process, the poem begins "fluently," "feverishly," in a "mysterious life process." Once written, however, words become objects, suitable for evaluation with "reasons," by the "will" and the "intellect." *Both* abilities have roles in the creation of the poem:

> I am not speaking of two persons, a poet and a critic, I am speaking of the same person, the writer. He has written with his deepest mind, now the object is there and he is attacking it with his most recent mind, the fore-brain, the seat of memory . . . the so-called intelligence.[14]

It is because Williams considered criticism an essential part of poetry that one cannot overlook its role in his own work. His attention to craft made him cognizant of the problems of poetic theory; it also made of him a perceptive critic in his own right.

In addition to Williams' critical sense and his natural poetic gifts, he possessed a third valuable quality, that of artistic humility. Never afraid to experiment in public, he often made himself the target for unfavorable comment. He did so because he recognized that poetry was in a state of transition and therefore needed the experimentation of all poets. He felt that only by sharing theories and results could contemporary poets further their art. Considering himself but a single member in the universal community of artists, Williams evaluated his work characteristically: "What I want to emphasize is that I do not consider anything I have put down there as final. There will be other experiments."[15]

Of similar intention were his constant efforts to encourage young writers. Williams' letters of sympathetic advice, his critiques and introductions (often too generous in emphasizing a single virtue to the neglect of all faults), his willingness to contribute to any little magazine or new press—all show his eager interest in the future of poetry. Many of his critical theories were first expressed in answer to another poet's request or as a lecture for students. One of Williams' last self-portraits depicts the poet as an old man whose chief interest still lay in "trying/ to get the young/ to foreshorten/ their errors in the use of words."

Devotion to his fellow men was nothing new for Williams, as his medical career had shown. That he could be both poet and doctor often amazed observers, yet the two professions—at least as Williams practiced them—had many similarities. Both required the desire to help mankind, often at great personal expense. Both required disciplined skill: just as he did advanced study in medicine so Williams considered the techniques of poetry his "Bible." And both dealt ultimately with basic human need.

Williams' dual vocation may very well have been possible because
he had early decided that his role in life was "to repair, to rescue, to
complete."[16] As a poet no less than as a physician, he had countless
opportunities to give aid:

> It is difficult
> to get the news from poems
> yet men die miserably every day
> for lack
> of what is found there.
> Hear me out
> for I too am concerned
> and every man
> who wants to die at peace in his bed . . .
> ("Asphodel," *Pictures,* pp. 161-162.)

By conveying truths unapproachable through science or logic, poetry
liberates men. It also "closes up the ranks of understanding," and "is
the solvent—or it can be—of old antagonisms."[17]

A means of communicating truth, of uniting men who are commonly divided, of re-creating a living culture, art to Williams was the
only panacea for the ills of contemporary society. As his 1950 definition of poetry shows, however, he realized that the good poem was in-
expressibly difficult to achieve:

> The poem to me (until I go broke) is an attempt, an experiment,
> a failing experiment, toward assertion with broken means but an
> assertion, always, of a new and total culture, the lifting of an en-
> vironment to expression. Thus it is social, the poem is a social in-
> strument—accepted or not accepted seems to be of no material
> importance. It embraces everything we are.
> The poem (for I never if possible speak of poetry) is the asser-
> tion that we are alive as ourselves . . .

And with his recurring late emphasis on "theme," Williams concluded
this definition with the comment that "there is a theme which is greater
than any poem or any poet worthy of following—or if not, there's not
much use bothering about what a poem 'means.' "[18] In Williams'
work, his insistence on his own contemporary local makes vividly
meaningful his traditional theme of man's relation to man and to his
world, a theme emerging clearly despite the "broken means" of
language.

In a final analysis, the poetry of William Carlos Williams proves
that he made what will undoubtedly be a lasting assertion—an attain-

ment consistent with his life-long belief in the local, in the language of natural speech, and in the poem as an imitation of the best of both. To a less devoted artist, the cost of his accomplishment would have been prohibitive. Half a century of diligent practice honed Williams' poetic skills into the tools of a master craftsman, tools tempered to brilliance in the exhausting fires of creative genius. But no cost was too high for him, convinced as he was that "The work an artist has to do is the most important creation of civilization. It is also its creator."[19]

Notes

INTRODUCTION

1. Letter to Harvey Breit, March 18, 1942, in *The Selected Letters of William Carlos Williams*, ed. John C. Thirlwall (New York: McDowell, Obolensky, 1957), p. 194. This work is hereafter cited as *Letters*. Quoted with the permission of the publishers; copyright © 1957 by William Carlos Williams.

2. "Against the Weather," in *Selected Essays of William Carlos Williams* (New York: Random House, 1954), pp. 197-199. This work is hereafter cited as *Essays*. Quoted with the permission of the publishers; copyright © 1931, 1936, 1938, 1939, 1940, 1942, 1946, 1948, 1949, 1951, 1954 by William Carlos Williams.

3. In this study, *principles* designates the constant beliefs of the poet, those central to his art; *corollaries,* the changing technical theories which grew from the principles but reflected the changing local.

4. Vivienne Koch, *William Carlos Williams* (Norfolk, Conn.: New Directions, 1950), pp. 261, 1.

5. Because many early single books are out of print, the volumes of poems used are those most readily available: *The Collected Earlier Poems of William Carlos Williams*, 1951; *The Collected Later Poems of William Carlos Williams,* 1963; *Pictures from Brueghel,* which contains *The Desert Music* and *Journey to Love,* 1962; and *Paterson* I-V, 1963.

CHAPTER ONE

1. *This Modern Poetry* (New York: W. W. Norton and Co., 1935), p. 70.

2. "Thing Is the Form," *The Nation,* CLXXVIII (April 24, 1954), 369.

3. April 12, 1950, in *Letters,* p. 286.

4. Quoted by Vivienne Koch, *op. cit.,* p. 263.

5. Unpublished letter to the editor of the *Quarterly Review of Literature,* pp. 1-2, in William Carlos Williams papers, Collection of American Literature, Yale University Library, New Haven, Connecticut. Material from this collection is hereafter cited as Yale Collection.

6. Unpublished typescripts entitled "Axioms," in William Carlos Williams papers, Lockwood Memorial Library Poetry Collection, State University of New York at Buffalo, New York. Material from this collection is hereafter cited as UB Collection.

7. *In the American Grain* (Norfolk, Conn.: New Directions, 1956), p. 33. Originally published in New York by Albert and Charles Boni, 1925. Reprinted with the permission of New Directions; copyright © 1925 by James Laughlin, 1933 by William Carlos Williams.

8. *Ibid.,* p. 109.

9. Letter to T. C. Wilson, March 10, 1932, in *Letters,* p. 120.

10. Unpublished letter to James Laughlin, January 20, 1939, Yale Collection.

11. Quoted by Norman Holmes Pearson, "Williams, New Jersey," *The Literary Review,* I (Autumn 1957), 36.

12. *The Collected Later Poems of William Carlos Williams* (Norfolk, Conn.: New Directions, 1963), p. 5. This work is hereafter cited as *CLP*. Quoted with the permission of the publisher; copyright © 1944, 1948, 1950, 1963 by William Carlos Williams.

13. Quoted by John C. Thirlwall, "William Carlos Williams' *Paterson:* The Search for the Redeeming Language—A Personal Epic in Five Parts," *New Directions 17* (1961), pp. 253-254.

14. Letter to Harriet Monroe, March 5, 1913, in *Letters,* p. 25.

15. "The Poem as a Field of Action," *Essays,* p. 284.

16. "Comment," *Essays,* pp. 28-29.

17. Letter to Henry Wells, April 12, 1950, in *Letters,* p. 286.

18. "Caviar and Bread Again: A Warning to the New Writer," *Essays,* p. 103.

19. "The Basis of Faith in Art," *Essays,* p. 195.

20. William Carlos Williams, "New Poetical Economy," *Poetry,* II (July, 1934), 221-222.

21. "Carl Sandburg's *Complete Poems,*" *Essays,* p. 272. Because Williams wrote truthfully when he said that Whitman was "a key man to whom I keep returning," the following are only a few of the sources of his commentary on that poet: "An Approach to the Poem," *English Institute Essays, 1947* (New York: Columbia University Press, 1948), p. 62; "Against the Weather," *Essays,* pp. 212, 218; "On Measure—Statement for Cid Corman," *Essays,* p. 339; "An Essay on *Leaves of*

Grass," Leaves of Grass: One Hundred Years After, ed. Milton Hindus (Stanford, California: Stanford University Press, 1955), pp. 22-31.

22. "A Study of Ezra Pound's Present Position," dated 1/21/47, Yale Collection. See also *Letters,* p. 264.

23. Notes from Williams' Briarcliff Junior College talk, p. 9. Roll 22, Microfilm, UB Collection.

24. *CLP,* p. 4.

25. "Against the Weather," *Essays,* p. 198.

26. March 5, 1913, *Letters,* p. 24.

27. Walter Sutton, "A Visit with William Carlos Williams," *Minnesota Review,* I (1961), 321.

28. Letter to Oswald LeWinter, 10/10/53, in *Letters,* p. 319.

29. Letter to Ronald Latimer, November 26, 1934, in *Letters,* p. 151.

30. Williams termed this first long poem, written in 1908 and 1909, "My big opus, the *Endymion*-like romantic poem" (*The Autobiography of William Carlos Williams,* New York: Random House, 1951, p. 106). He described its medieval setting, the deaths of the royal family, and the wanderings of the prince. The opus was written in couplets, sonnets, and blank verse (pp. 59-60). Quoted by permission of the publishers; copyright © 1948, 1949, 1951 by William Carlos Williams.

31. William Carlos Williams, *Poems* (Rutherford, New Jersey: Reid Howell, 1909), p. 15.

32. *Poetry,* I (1913), 200-206.

33. Williams' Dartmouth lecture, p. 8. Unpublished typescripts, UB Collection.

34. William Carlos Williams, *The Great American Novel,* in *American Short Novels,* ed. R. P. Blackmur (New York: Thomas Y. Crowell Co., 1960), p. 315. Originally published by The Three Mountains Press, Paris, 1923.

35. "Yours, O Youth," *Essays,* pp. 33-36.

36. Letter to Robert McAlmon, in *Letters,* p. 57.

37. October 3, 1938, in *Letters,* p. 173.

38. Unpublished typescripts, sections dated 2/5/41, p. 1, UB Collection.

39. "The Poem as a Field of Action," *Essays,* pp. 282-283.

40. *Ibid.,* p. 281.

41. *Ibid.,* p. 286.

42. Charles Olson, *Projective Verse* (Brooklyn: Totem Press, 1959).

43. Letter to Kay Boyle, 1932, in *Letters,* p. 133.

44. "Poetry, Myth, and Reality," *The Language of Poetry,* ed. Allen Tate (Princeton, New Jersey: Princeton University Press, 1942), p. 3.
45. *The Greek Way to Western Civilization* (New York: The New American Library of World Literature, Inc., 1948), pp. 50-51.
46. "Prologue to *Kora in Hell*," *Essays,* p. 10.

CHAPTER TWO

1. *Autobiography,* p. 390.
2. "William Carlos Williams, Poet Who Cannot Pause," *New Republic,* CXXXV (September 17, 1956), 18.
3. "Introduction," *Essays,* pp. 232-234.
4. *CLP,* p. 99. See also William Carlos Williams, *I Wanted to Write a Poem,* ed. Edith Heal (Boston: Beacon Press, 1958), p. 21. Reprinted by permission of the publishers; copyright © 1958 by William Carlos Williams.
5. "Notes in Diary Form," *Essays,* p. 62.
6. Unpublished typescripts, "The Basis of Faith in Art," p. 5. UB Collection.
7. Sutton, "A Visit with William Carlos Williams," p. 322.
8. William Carlos Williams, "Faiths for a Complex World," *The American Scholar,* XXVI (Fall 1957), 457.
9. "The Poem as a Field of Action," *Essays,* p. 282.
10. "Against the Weather," *Essays,* p. 196.
11. *The Metamorphic Tradition in Modern Poetry* (New Brunswick, New Jersey: Rutgers University Press, 1955), p. 8.
12. *The Collected Earlier Poems of William Carlos Williams* (Norfolk, Conn.: New Directions, 1951), p. 33. This work is hereafter cited as *CEP.* Quoted with the permission of the publisher; copyright © 1938, 1951 by William Carlos Williams.
13. Letter to Alva N. Turner, October 27, 1920, in *Letters,* pp. 46-47.
14. *Autobiography,* p. 158.
15. Letter to Norman Holmes Pearson, November 7, 1938, in *Letters,* p. 175.
16. Letter to Alfred Stieglitz, June 27, 1937, in *Letters,* p. 168.
17. Letter to Horace Gregory, May 9, 1944, in *Letters,* pp. 227-228.
18. Letter to Robert McAlmon, May 25, 1939, in *Letters,* p. 181.
19. Notes for "A Note on the Turn of the View Toward Poetic Technique," written for *The Hanover Forum,* V, No. 1, Yale Collection.

20.   Letter to Robert McAlmon, February 23, 1944, in *Letters*, p. 222.

21.   Letter to William Eric Williams, September 25, 1942, in *Letters*, p. 202.

22.   William Carlos Williams, "To a Dog Injured in the Street," *Pictures from Brueghel and Other Poems* (Norfolk, Conn.: New Directions, 1962), p. 88. This work is hereafter cited as *Pictures*. Quoted with the permission of the publishers; copyright © 1949, 1951, 1952, 1953, 1954, 1955, 1956, 1957, 1959, 1960, 1961, 1962 by William Carlos Williams.

CHAPTER THREE

1.   *Essays*, p. xii.

2.   "A Note on the Recent Work of James Joyce," *Essays*, p. 75.

3.   *The Primary Language of Poetry in the 1940's* (Berkeley: University of California Press, 1951), p. 439.

4.   *Ibid.*, pp. 455-456.

5.   *Cobras and Cockle Shells: Modes in Recent Poetry* (Flushing, New York: The Sparrow Press, 1958), pp. 32-44.

6.   Letter to Ezra Pound, August 11, 1928, in *Letters*, p. 105.

7.   "A Note on Layton," introduction to Irving Layton's *The Improved Binoculars* (Highlands, North Carolina: Jonathan Williams, 1956), n.p.

8.   Dr. Williams' closing note to Louis Zukofsky's *"A" 1–12* (Ashland, Mass.: Origin Press, 1959), p. 291.

9.   "A Note on Layton," n.p.

10.   Reprinted by permission of the publishers, Shakespeare Head Press, Eton, England.

11.   *The Primary Language of Poetry in the 1940's*, p. 446.

12.   Letter to T. C. Wilson, December 22, 1933, in unpublished letters, Yale Collection.

13.   Williams' notes for a review of Kenneth Rexroth's *In Defense of the Earth*, p. 3. Yale Collection.

14.   In a speech about *Paterson*, August 6, 1953. As recorded by Thirlwall in "Appendix IV" of "William Carlos Williams' *Paterson*," *New Directions 17*, p. 309.

15.   Williams' notes for a review of Louis Zukofsky's *55 Poems*, p. 3. Yale Collection.

16.   Letter to Kenneth Burke, January 26, 1933, in "The Letters of William Carlos Williams," *The Golden Goose*, VII (April 1954), 128.

17.   "Prologue to *Kora in Hell*," *Essays*, p. 16.

18.   *In Defense of Ignorance* (New York: Random House, 1952), p. 156.
19.   Letter to Kenneth Burke, 1947, in *Letters,* p. 257.

CHAPTER FOUR

1.   "Preface to a Book of Poems," p. 3. Unpublished typescript, UB Collection.
2.   First complete draft (May 23, 1944) of Williams' "Commentary" to his translation of Quevado's *The Dog and the Fever,* p. 19. Yale Collection.
3.   "Marianne Moore," *Essays,* p. 122.
4.   "Poet Who Cannot Pause," p. 18.
5.   William Carlos Williams, *Paterson,* I-V (Norfolk, Conn.: New Directions, 1963), p. 262. Quoted with the permission of the publisher; copyright © 1946, 1948, 1949, 1951, 1958 by William Carlos Williams; copyright © 1963 by Florence Williams.
6.   "Revelation," *Essays,* p. 268.
7.   *I Wanted to Write a Poem,* p. 73.
8.   Briarcliff Junior College talk, p. 3. Unpublished typescripts, UB Collection.
9.   Letter to Oswald LeWinter, October 10, 1953, in *Letters,* p. 319.
10.   Letter to Norman Macleod, July 25, 1945, in *Letters,* p. 239.
11.   Letter to Louis Martz, May 27, 1951, in *Letters,* p. 298.
12.   *Cobras and Cockle Shells,* p. 43.
13.   Sutton, "A Visit with William Carlos Williams," p. 321. *Pictures from Brueghel* includes poems written as early as 1953, showing that, even in the midst of his work with the triadic line, Williams was composing these shorter poems which need not "say anything."
14.   Manuscripts of "The American Spirit in Art," pp. 4-5. Yale Collection.

CHAPTER FIVE

1.   In a talk with John C. Thirlwall, 1953, as recorded by the latter in "Ten Years of a New Rhythm," *Pictures from Brueghel,* p. 183.
2.   Quoted by John C. Thirlwall in "The Lost Poems of William Carlos Williams," *New Directions 16* (1957), p. 26.
3.   Letter to Miss Monroe, March 5, 1913, in *Letters,* p. 24.
4.   *I Wanted to Write a Poem,* p. 18.
5.   *Letters,* p. 24.
6.   Letter to Harriet Monroe, October 26, 1916, *Letters,* p. 39.

7. As recorded on "William Carlos Williams Reads His Poetry," Caedmon records, New York, 1958.

8. *I Wanted to Write a Poem,* p. 66.

9. "Preface," *Quarterly Review of Literature,* II, No. 4 (1944), p. 349.

10. Letter to Kenneth Burke, 1947, in *Letters,* pp. 257-258.

11. *I Wanted to Write a Poem,* p. 74.

12. Draft of "A Study of Pound," Yale Collection.

13. "An Approach to the Poem," *English Institute Essays, 1947,* p. 47.

14. "Letter on Pound," *Quarterly Review of Literature,* V, No. 3 (1950), 301.

15. Sutton, "A Visit with William Carlos Williams," pp. 309-310.

16. Letter to Louis Martz, May 27, 1951, in *Letters,* p. 299.

17. Letter to Marianne Moore, June 23, 1951, in *Letters,* p. 305.

18. Letter to John Thirlwall, June 13, 1955, in *Letters,* p. 334.

19. Letter to Richard Eberhart, May 23, 1954, in *Letters,* p. 327.

20. Robert Lowell, "William Carlos Williams," *Hudson Review,* XIV (Winter 1961-62), 533-534.

21. Kenneth Rexroth, "A Poet Sums Up," *New York Times Books* (March 28, 1954), 5.

22. Sutton, "A Visit with William Carlos Williams," 310.

23. Microfilmed notes for *Paterson,* section entitled "The Principle of Literary Composition," p. 50. UB Collection.

24. Letter to Robert Lowell, March 11, 1952, in *Letters,* p. 313.

CHAPTER SIX

1. *Autobiography,* p. 392.

2. Williams speaking to John C. Thirlwall, August 6, 1953. Recorded by Mr. Thirlwall in "Appendix IV" to "William Carlos Williams' *Paterson,*" *New Directions 17,* p. 309.

3. Unpublished notes for *Paterson,* Yale Collection.

4. Letter to Marianne Moore, November 7, 1944, in *Letters,* p. 232.

5. Williams speaking to John C. Thirlwall, April 8, 1954. Recorded by Mr. Thirlwall in "William Carlos Williams' *Paterson,*" *New Directions 17,* p. 277.

6. *Autobiography,* p. 391.

7. *Poetry and the Age* (New York: Alfred A. Knopf, 1953), p. 261.

8. "Poet Americanus," *The Commonweal,* LXX (September 18, 1959), 520.

9. " 'I Will Teach You My Townspeople,' " *The Kenyon Review*, XII (Autumn 1950), 538.

10. "Modern Verse: Diffusion as a Principle of Composition," *The Kenyon Review*, XXI (Spring 1959), 200.

11. "America Revisited," *Poetry*, XC (August 1957), 316-317.

12. *The Metamorphic Tradition in Modern Poetry*, p. 8.

13. Williams speaking to John C. Thirlwall as recorded in "Appendix IV," "William Carlos Williams' *Paterson*," *New Directions 17*, p. 309.

14. *Ibid.*, p. 307.

15. *Ibid.*

16. *I Wanted to Write a Poem*, p. 22.

17. Unpublished notes on "Asphodel," Yale Collection.

18. Unpublished poems, "Tribute to the poet Neruda": Yale Collection:

    Now that I am all but blind, . . .
                    the imagination
    has turned inward as happened
    to my mother when she
    was old: dreams took the
    place of sight . . . .

19. Williams' draft of "A Note on the Turn of the View Toward Poetic Technique," Yale Collection.

20. "The Adoration of Kings," *Pictures*, p. 6.

21. Unpublished notes for *Paterson*, Yale Collection.

22. Unpublished manuscript of "Asphodel," Yale Collection.

23. Unpublished manuscript of "The Desert Music," Yale Collection.

24. Microfilmed notes for *Paterson*, p. 33; UB Collection.

25. "The Unicorn in *Paterson:* William Carlos Williams," *Thought*, XXXV (Winter 1960), 546-547.

26. *In the American Grain*, p. 121.

27. Unpublished notes for *Paterson*, Yale Collection.

28. Unpublished letter to Louis Zukofsky, May 29, 1943, Yale Collection.

29. *I Wanted to Write a Poem*, p. 64.

30. Letter to Parker Tyler, March 10, 1948, in *Letters*, p. 263.

31. Unpublished letter to James Laughlin, June 16, 1941, Yale Collection.

32. Unpublished notes for *Paterson*, Yale Collection.

33. *Ibid.*

34. Unpublished letter to Dick, undated, Yale Collection.

35. Statement on the poet, taken from "Symposium on Writing," *The Golden Goose,* Series III, No. 2 (Autumn 1951), 90-91.

36. Manuscripts of "Emanuel Romano," p. 8. Yale Collection.

37. Manuscripts of "The Function of Literature: An Address To Be Given Before the Institute of Humanistic Studies for Executives of the University of Pennsylvania Program for Junior Executives of the Bell Telephone Companies," p. 14. Yale Collection.

CHAPTER SEVEN

1. "A Poet Sums Up," *New York Times Books* (March 28, 1954), 5.

2. Briarcliff Junior College talk, p. 10. Roll 22, Microfilm, UB Collection.

3. Dartmouth lecture, n.p. Roll 22, Microfilm, UB Collection.

4. *Letters,* p. 298.

5. *Many Loves and Other Plays* (Norfolk, Conn.: New Directions, 1961), pp. 8-9. Quoted with the permission of the publisher; copyright © 1936, 1942, 1948, 1961 by William Carlos Williams.

6. Quoted by Robert Halsband in " 'I Lived Among These People,' " *Saturday Review,* XXXIII (December 9, 1950), 14.

7. Manuscripts of "The American Spirit in Art," p. 5. Yale Collection.

8. Unpublished letter of Denise Levertov to William Carlos Williams, June 18, 1962, p. 2. Printed with the permission of Miss Levertov. Yale Collection.

9. "The High Bridge above the Tagus River at Toledo," *Pictures,* p. 53.

10. Worksheets, Yale Collection.

11. Unpublished notes for *Paterson,* Yale Collection.

12. Letter to James Laughlin, January 6, 1941, in "Four Unpublished Letters by William Carlos Williams," *The Massachusetts Review,* III, No. 2 (Winter 1962), 293.

13. Notes for a review of Sandburg's *Complete Poems,* Yale Collection.

14. "How To Write," pp. 1-5. Unpublished typescripts, UB Collection.

15. "On Measure—Statement for Cid Corman," *Essays,* p. 340.

16. Letter to Marianne Moore, May 2, 1934, in *Letters,* p. 147.

17. "Against the Weather," *Essays,* p. 198.

18. Letter to Henry Wells, April 12, 1950, in *Letters,* p. 286.

19. "Against the Weather," *Essays,* p. 197.

How To Write

By William Carlos Williams*

ONE takes a piece of paper, anything, the flat of a shingle, slate, cardboard and with anything handy to the purpose begins to put down the words after the desired expression in mind. This is the anarchical phase of writing. The blankness of the writing surface may cause the mind to shy, it may be impossible to release the faculties. Write, write anything: it is all in all probability worthless anyhow, it is never hard to destroy written characters. But it is absolutely essential to the writing of anything worth while that the mind be fluid and release itself to the task.

Forget all rules, forget all restrictions, as to taste, as to what ought to be said, write for the pleasure of it—whether slowly or fast—every form of resistance to a complete release should be abandoned.

For today we know the meaning of depth, it is a primitive profoundity of the personality that must be touched if what we do is to have it. The faculties, untied, proceed backward through the night of our unconscious past. It goes down to the ritualistic, amoral past of the race, to fetish, to dream to wherever the "genius" of the particular writer finds itself able to go.

At such a time the artist (the writer) may well be thought of as a dangerous person. Anything may turn up. He has no connection with ordered society. He may perform an imbecility or he may by a freak of mind penetrate with tremendous value to society into some avenue long closed or never yet opened. But he is disconnected with any orderly advance or purpose.

It is now that artists stoutly defend themselves against any usefulness in their art. And it makes no difference whether it is a treatise on mathematics or a poem that is being written. *While* it is being written, as far as possible, the writer be he mathematician or poet, must with a stored mind no doubt, must nevertheless thoroughly abandon himself to the writing in greater or less degree if he wishes to clinch his expression with any depth of significance.

The demonic power of the mind is its racial and individual past, it is the rhythmic ebb and flow of the mysterious life process and unless this is tapped by the writer nothing of moment can result. It is the reason for the value of poetry whose unacknowledged rhythmic symbolism is its greatest strength and which makes all prose in comparison with it little more than the patter of the intelligence.

So poets have been considered unbalanced creatures (as they often are), madmen very often. But the intrinsic reason for this is seldom understood. They are in touch with "voices", but this is the very essence of their power, the voices are the past, the depths of our very beings. It is the deeper, not "lower" (in the usually silly sense) portions of the personality speaking, the middle brain, the nerves, the glands, the very muscles and bones of the body itself speaking.

But once the writing is on the paper it becomes an object. It is no longer a fluid speaking through a symbolism of ritualistic forms but definite words on a piece of paper. It has now left the region of the formative past and come up to the present. It has entered now a new field, that of intelligence. I do not say that the two fields do not somewhat overlap at times but the chief characteristic of the writing now is that it is an object for the liveliest attention that the full mind can give it and that there has been a change in the whole situation.

It is this part of writing that is dealt with in the colleges and in all forms of teaching but nowhere does it seem to be realized that without its spring from the deeper strata of the personality all the teaching and learning in the world can make nothing of the result. Not to have realized this is the greatest fault of those who think they know something of the art.

All that the first phase of writing has accomplished is to place its record on the paper. Is this valuable, is it worthless? These questions it cannot answer and it is of no use for the poet to say: This is what *I* have done, therefore it is excellent. He may say that and what he has done may be excellent but the reasons should be made clear and they involve the conscious intelligence.

The written object comes under the laws of all created things involving a choice and once the choice has been made there must be an exercise of the will to back it. One goes forward carefully. But the first step must not be to make what has been written under a quasi-hallu-cinatory state conform to rules. What rules? Rather the writing should be carefully examined for the new and the extraordinary and nothing rejected without clear reason. For in this way the intelligence itself is corrected.

Thus, we know that in language is anchored most of all of the wis-dom and follies of our lives. Besides which language may grow stale, meanings may and will be lost, phrases may block our arrival at con-clusion. And in the writings of genius, in the poems (if any) the re-leased personality of the artist the very break with stupidity which we are seeking may have occurred. And this will always be in the *form* which the first writing has taken.

But lest a mistake occur I am not speaking of two persons, a poet and a critic, I am speaking of the same person, the writer. He has written with his deepest mind, now the object is there and he is attack-ing it with his most recent mind, the fore-brain, the seat of memory and ratiocination, the so-called intelligence.

This cannot do more in reviewing that which is before it than reject that which has been said better elsewhere. Whereas in the first phase a man need not seriously have written at all, now it is necessary that he know the work of other men, in other times, as much as possible and from every available angle. This is the student's moment.

And for an American there is one great decision to be made. What language is being written?

A few years ago some American in England wrote an attack upon American writers living in America saying in effect; How can they write English not hearing it spoken every day?—His comment was meant to be ironical but it turned out to be naive. The answer to his question is, naturally: Why bother with English when we have a lan-guage of our own?

It is the intelligence which gives us the history of writing and its point of arrival today, the place of Poe, the value of Whitman, the purpose of free verse, why it occurred at just that time, the significance of Gertrude Stein's work, that of the writings of James Joyce and the rationale of modern verse structure.

Briefly all this is the birth of a new language. It is a new allotment of significance. It is the cracking up of phrases which have stopped the mind.

All these things could be gone into in detail, a book could be written and must be written of them, but that is not my purpose here. What I have undertaken is to show the two great phases of writing without either of which the work accomplished can hardly be called mastery. And that, in the phrase of James Joyce, is the he and the she of it.

Selected Bibliography

I. Primary Sources

Williams, William Carlos. "The American Idiom," *New Directions 17* (1961), 250-251.

———. "An Approach to the Poem," *English Institute Essays, 1947.* New York: Columbia University Press, 1948, pp. 50-76.

———. *The Autobiography of William Carlos Williams.* New York: Random House, 1951.

———. Introduction to Ronald Bayes' *Dust and Desire.* Devon, England: Arthur L. Stockwell, Lmt., 1960.

———. *The Build Up.* New York: Random House, 1952.

———. "Cézanne," *The Nation,* CXCII (May 13, 1961), 416.

———. *The Collected Earlier Poems of William Carlos Williams.* Norfolk, Conn.: New Directions, 1951.

———. *The Collected Later Poems of William Carlos Williams.* Norfolk, Conn.: New Directions, 1963.

———. Foreword to Tram Combs' *Pilgrims' Terrace.* San Germán, Puerto Rico: La Nueva Solamanca, 1957.

———. *Contact,* I-V, ed. William Carlos Williams and Robert McAlmon. 1920-1923.

———. *Contact,* I-III, ed. William Carlos Williams and Nathaneal West. 1932.

———. *The Desert Music.* New York: Random House, 1954.

———. "An Essay on *Leaves of Grass,*" *Leaves of Grass: One Hundred Years After,* ed. Milton Hindus. Stanford, California: Stanford University Press, 1955, pp. 22-31.

———. "Experimental and Formal Verse: Some Hints Toward the Enjoyment of Modern Verse," *Quarterly Review of Literature,* VIII, No. 3 (1953), 171-175.

———. "Faiths for a Complex World," *American Scholar,* XXVI (Fall 1957), 453-457.

———. *The Farmer's Daughters*. Norfolk, Conn.: New Directions, 1961. Introduction by Van Wyck Brooks.

———. "The Fatal Blunder," *Quarterly Review of Literature*, II, No. 2 (1944), 125-127.

———. "The First President," *The New Caravan*, ed. Alfred Kreymborg et al. New York: W. W. Norton and Co., 1936.

———. "5 to the 5th Power," *New Republic*, CXXXVI (January 21, 1957), 20.

———. "From: A Folded Skyscraper," *The American Caravan*, ed. Alfred Kreymborg et al. New York: The Macaulay Co., 1927.

———. "From Queens to Cats," *The Dial*, LXXXVI (January 1929), 66-67.

———. "The Future of the Creative Arts," *University of Buffalo Studies*, XIX, No. 4 (February 1952), 10-12.

———. Introduction to Allen Ginsberg's *Empty Mirror*. New York: Totem Press, 1961.

———. Introduction to Allen Ginsberg's *Howl and Other Poems*. San Francisco: City Lights Books, 1956.

———. "Good . . . For What?" *The Dial*, LXXXVI (March 1929), 250-252.

———. *The Great American Novel* in *American Short Novels*, ed. R. P. Blackmur. New York: Thomas Y. Crowell Co., 1960, pp. 307-344. Originally published by The Three Mountains Press, Paris, 1923.

———. "Homage to Ford Madox Ford," *New Directions 7* (1942), 490-491.

———. "How To Write," *New Directions 1936*. Norfolk, Conn.: New Directions, 1936.

———. *I Wanted to Write a Poem*, ed. Edith Heal. Boston: Beacon Press, 1958.

———. "Impasse and Imagery," *The Dial*, LXXXV (November 1928), 431-433.

———. "In Praise of Marriage," *Quarterly Review of Literature*, II, No. 2 (1944), 145-149.

———. *In the American Grain*. Norfolk, Conn.: New Directions, 1956. Originally published by Albert and Charles Boni, New York, 1925.

———. *In the Money*. Norfolk, Conn.: New Directions, 1940.

———. *Journey to Love*. New York: Random House, 1955.

———. Foreword to Robert E. Knoll's *Robert McAlmon*. Lincoln, Nebraska: University of Nebraska Press, 1959.

———. *Kora in Hell: Improvisations*. San Francisco: City Lights

Books, 1957. Originally published by The Four Seas Co., Boston, 1920.

——. "A Note on Layton," introduction to Irving Layton's *The Improved Binoculars*. Highlands, North Carolina: Jonathan Williams, 1956.

——. "Letter on Pound," *Quarterly Review of Literature*, V, No. 3 (1950), 301.

——. "Letter to an Australian Editor," *Briarcliff Quarterly*, III (October 1946), 205-209.

——. "The Letters of William Carlos Williams," *The Golden Goose*, No. 7 (April 1954), 124-132.

——. Introduction to Ronald Loewinsohn's *Watermelons*. New York: Totem Press, 1959.

——. *Many Loves and Other Plays*. Norfolk, Conn.: New Directions, 1961.

——. "Marianne Moore," *The Dial*, LXXVIII (May 1925), 393-401.

——. "Marianne Moore," *Quarterly Review of Literature*, IV, No. 1 (1946), 125-127.

——. "Measure," *Spectrum* (Fall 1959), 152-153.

——. "Men . . . Have No Tenderness," *New Directions 7* (1942), 429-436.

——. Microfilms of Dr. Williams' Manuscripts, Rolls 21-26. Lockwood Memorial Library Poetry Collection, State University of New York at Buffalo, Buffalo, New York.

——. Microfilms of Dr. Williams' Notes for *Paterson*, unnumbered. Lockwood Memorial Library Poetry Collection, State University of New York at Buffalo, Buffalo, New York.

——. Preface to Merrill Moore's *The Dance of Death*. Brooklyn: I. E. Rubin, 1957.

——. "The Moral," *Poetry*, CIII, No. 4 (January 1964), 254.

——. "A New Line Is a New Measure," *The New Quarterly of Poetry*, I, No. 2 (Winter 1947-48), 8-16.

——. "The New Poetical Economy," *Poetry*, XLIV (July 1934), 220-225.

——. "Note on University Instruction in the Nature of the Poem," *The Golden Goose*, No. 3 (June 1949), 29-30.

——. "Notes from a Talk on Poetry," *Poetry*, XIV (July 1919), 211-216.

——. *A Novelette and Other Prose, 1921-31*. Toulon, France: Imprimerie F. Cabasson, 1932.

——. "On Burke," *The Dial*, LXXXVI (January 1929), 6-8.

——. *Paterson*. Norfolk, Conn.: New Directions, 1963. Originally published in single volumes by New Directions, 1946, 1948, 1949, 1951, and 1958.

———. *Picasso the Figure.* New York: Louis Carré Gallery, 1950.

———. *Pictures from Brueghel and Other Poems.* Norfolk, Conn.: New Directions, 1962. Includes *The Desert Music* and *Journey to Love.*

———. *Poems.* Rutherford, New Jersey: Reid Howell (privately printed), 1909.

———. "Poet Who Cannot Pause," *New Republic,* CXXXV (September 17, 1956), 18.

———. "Preface," *Quarterly Review of Literature,* II, No. 4 (1944), 346-350.

———. "Review of *95 Poems,*" *Evergreen Review,* II, No. 7 (Winter 1959), 214-217.

———. *The Selected Essays of William Carlos Williams.* New York: Random House, 1954.

———. *The Selected Letters of William Carlos Williams,* ed. John C. Thirlwall, New York: McDowell, Obolensky, 1957.

———. *The Selected Poems of William Carlos Williams.* Norfolk, Conn.: New Directions, 1963. Introduction by Randall Jarrell.

———. "70 Years Deep," *Holiday,* XVI (November 1954), 54-55.

———. Letter from Dr. Williams to Martha Baird, November 7, 1951, used as introduction to *Hot Afternoons Have Been in Montana: Poems by Eli Siegel.* New York: Definition Press, 1957.

———. "Some Notes toward an Autobiography," *Poetry,* LXXII (June 1948), 147-155; (August 1948), 264-270; LXXIV (May 1949), 94-111.

———. *Spring and All.* Dijon, France: Contact Publishing Company, 1923.

———. "Stormy," *Poetry,* CI, Nos. 1-2 (October-November 1962), 141.

———. "Symposium on Writing," *The Golden Goose,* Series 3, No. 2 (Autumn 1951), 89-96.

———. Taped recordings of Dr. Williams reading from his poems. Four tapes, Collection of American Literature, Yale University Library, New Haven, Conn.

———. "A Tribute," *John Marin.* Berkeley: University of California Press, 1956.

———. Unpublished manuscripts. Lockwood Memorial Library Poetry Collection, State University of New York at Buffalo, Buffalo, New York.

———. "Verse with a Jolt to It," *New York Times Books* (January 28, 1951), p. 5.

———. *A Voyage to Pagany.* New York: The Macaulay Co., 1928.

———. *White Mule.* Norfolk, Conn.: New Directions, 1937.

———. "William Carlos Williams Reads His Poetry" (recording). New York: Caedmon Publishers, 1958.

———. "William Carlos Williams: Two Letters," *The Golden Goose,* IV, No. 5 (October 1952), 29-32.

———. William Carlos Williams' manuscripts and letters. Collection of American Literature, Yale University Library, New Haven, Conn.

———. *Yes, Mrs. Williams.* New York: McDowell, Obolensky, 1959.

———. Closing Note to Louis Zukofsky's *"A" 1-12.* Ashland, Mass.: Origin Press, 1959.

II. Secondary Sources

Aiken, Conrad P. *A Reviewer's ABC.* New York: Meridian Books, Inc., 1958.

Angoff, Charles. "3 Towering Figures," *The Literary Review,* VI, No. 4 (Summer 1963), 423-429.

Arnheim, Rudolf, W. H. Auden, Karl Shapiro, Donald A. Stauffer. *Poets at Work.* New York: Harcourt, Brace and Co., 1948.

Bennett, Joseph. "The Lyre and the Sledgehammer," *Hudson Review,* V, No. 2 (Summer 1952), 295-307.

Beum, Robert Lawrence. "The Baby Glove of a Pharoah," *Perspective,* VI, No. 4 (Autumn 1953), 217-223. (Issue devoted to articles on Dr. Williams.)

———. "The Neglect of Williams," *Poetry,* LXXX (August 1952), 291-293.

———. "The Recent Books of William Carlos Williams," *The Golden Goose,* IV, No. 5 (October 1952), 33-35.

Bittner, William and W. T. Scott. "William Carlos Williams: Muse or Patron Saint?" *Saturday Review,* XL (September 7, 1957), 13-14.

Blackmur, R. P. *Language as Gesture.* New York: Harcourt, Brace and Co., 1952.

Bogan, Louise. *Achievement in American Poetry, 1900-1950.* Chicago: Henry Regnery Co., 1951.

Brinnin, John Malcolm. *William Carlos Williams.* University of Minnesota Pamphlets on American Writers Series, No. 24. Minneapolis: University of Minnesota Press, 1963.

Burke, Kenneth. "Heaven's First Law," *The Dial,* LXXII (February 1922), 197-200.

————. "The Methods of William Carlos Williams," *The Dial*, LXXXII (February 1927), 94-98.

————. "William Carlos Williams, 1883-1963," *The New York Review of Books* (Spring-Summer 1963), 45-47.

Cambon, Glauco. *The Inclusive Flame: Studies in American Poetry.* Bloomington, Indiana: Indiana University Press, 1963.

Carruth, Hayden. "Dr. Williams' *Paterson*," *The Nation*, CLXX (April 8, 1950), 331-333.

————. "William Carlos Williams as One of Us," *New Republic*, CXLVIII (April 13, 1963), 30-32.

Ciardi, John. "The Epic of a Place," *Saturday Review*, XLI (October 11, 1958), 37-39.

————. "Thing Is the Form," *The Nation*, CLXXVIII (April 24, 1954), 368-369.

Coffman, Stanley K., Jr. *Imagism: A Chapter for the History of Modern Poetry.* Norman, Oklahoma: University of Oklahoma Press, 1951.

Cook, Albert. "Modern Verse: Diffusion as a Principle of Composition," *The Kenyon Review*, XXI (Spring 1959), 208-212.

Corman, Cid. *"The Farmer's Daughters:* A True Story about People," *The Massachusetts Review*, III, No. 2 (Winter 1962), 319-324. (Issue includes "A Gathering for William Carlos Williams," an extensive section of essays, poems, and pictures.)

Creeley, Robert. "The Fact of His Life," *The Nation*, CXCV (October 13, 1962), 224.

Deutsch, Babette. *Poetry in Our Time.* New York: Columbia University Press, 1956.

————. *This Modern Poetry.* New York: W. W. Norton and Co., 1935.

Dickey, James. "First and Last Things," *Poetry*, CIII, No. 5 (February 1964), 321-322.

Donoghue, Denis. "For a Redeeming Language," *Twentieth Century*, CLXIII (June 1958), 532-542.

Eberhart, Richard. "Book Review of *Collected Later Poems*," *New York Times Books* (December 17, 1950), 1.

————. "Prose, Poetry and the Love of Life," *Saturday Review*, CXXXVII (November 20, 1954), 20.

Eckman, Frederick. *Cobras and Cockle Shells: Modes in Recent Poetry.* Flushing, New York: The Sparrow Press, 1958.

————. "Modern Replicas," *The Golden Goose*, No. 2 (Autumn 1948), 36-38.

Emerson, Richard Wirtz. "The Recent Books of William Carlos Williams," *The Golden Goose*, IV, No. 5 (October 1952), 38-40.

Fiedler, Leslie. "Some Uses and Failures of Feeling," *Partisan Review*, XV, No. 2 (August 1948), 924-931.

Fiscalini, Janet. "Poet Americanus," *The Commonweal*, LXX (September 18, 1959), 519-521.

Fitzgerald, Robert. "Bejeweled, the Great Sun," *New Republic*, CXX (April 25, 1949), 22-23.

Flint, R. W. " 'I Will Teach You My Townspeople,' " *The Kenyon Review*, XII (Autumn 1950), 537-543.

Foster, John Lawrence. "The Modern American Long Poem," unpublished dissertation, University of Michigan, 1961.

Frankenberg, Lloyd. *Pleasure Dome: On Reading Modern Poetry.* Boston: Houghton Mifflin Co., 1949.

Franklyn, A. Fredric. "The Truth and the Poem," *Trace*, XII, No. 48 (Spring 1963), 32, 79-83.

Garrigue, Jean. "America Revisited," *Poetry*, XC (August 1957), 315-320.

Goll, Yvan. *Landless John: Jean Sans Terre*, trans. Lionel Able, Clark Mills, William Carlos Williams, John Gould Fletcher. San Francisco: The Grabhorn Press, 1944.

Goodman, Paul. "Between Flash and Thunderstroke," *Poetry*, LXXXVII (March 1956), 366-370.

Gregory, Horace and Marya Zaturenska. *A History of American Poetry: 1900-1940.* New York: Harcourt, Brace and Co., 1946.

Gregory, Horace. *The Shield of Achilles.* New York: Harcourt, Brace and Co., 1944.

———. "William Carlos Williams," *Life and Letters Today*, XXIV (February 1940), 164-176.

Halsband, Robert. " 'I Lived Among These People,' " *Saturday Review*, XXXIII (December 9, 1950), 14-15.

Hamilton, Edith. *The Greek Way to Western Civilization.* New York: The New American Library of World Literature, Inc., 1948. Originally published by W. W. Norton and Co., 1930.

Hartung, Charles. "A Poetry of Experience," *University of Kansas City Review*, XXV (October 1958), 65-69.

Hirschman, Jack. "William Carlos Williams," *Shenandoah*, XIV, No. 4 (Summer 1963), 3-10.

Hoffman, Frederick, J. "Williams and His Muse," *Poetry*, LXXXIV (April 1954), 23-27.

Honig, Edward. "City of Man," *Poetry*, LXIX (February 1947), 277-284.

———. "The *Paterson* Impasse," *Poetry*, LXXIV (April 1949), 37-41.

Ignatow, David. "Williams' Influence: Some Social Aspects," *Chelsea,* XIV (January 1964), 154–161.

Jacobsen, Josephine. "Legacy of Three Poets," *The Commonweal,* LXXVIII (May 10, 1963), 189-192.

Jarrell, Randall. "The Poet and His Public," *Partisan Review,* XIII (September-October 1946), 488-500.

———. *Poetry and the Age.* New York: Alfred A. Knopf, 1953.

———. "View of 3 Poets," *Partisan Review,* XVIII (November 1951), 698-700.

Kenner, Hugh. "Columbus Log-Book," *Poetry,* XCII (June 1958), 174-178.

———. "The Drama of Utterance," *The Massachusetts Review,* III, No. 2 (Winter 1962), 328-330.

———. *Gnomon.* New York: McDowell, Obolensky, 1958.

———. "To Measure Is All We Know," *Poetry,* XCIV (May 1959), 127-132.

———. "William Carlos Williams: In Memoriam," *National Review* (March 26, 1963), 237.

Koch, Vivienne. "The Man and the Poet," *The Kenyon Review,* XIV (Summer 1952), 502-510.

———. *William Carlos Williams.* Norfolk, Conn.: New Directions, 1950.

———. "Williams: The Social Mask," *Poetry,* LXXX (May 1954), 89-95.

Kreymborg, Alfred. *A History of American Poetry: Our Singing Strength.* New York: Tudor Publishing Co., 1934.

Kunitz, Stanley. "Frost, Williams, and Company," *Harpers,* CCXXV (October 1962), 100-103.

Lamott, Kenneth. "Pilgrimage to Rutherford," *Contact* (July 1963), 41-43.

Lechlitner, Ruth. "The Poetry of William Carlos Williams," *Poetry,* LIV (September 1939), 326-335.

Levertov, Denise. "William Carlos Williams," *The Nation,* CXCVI (March 16, 1963), 230.

Lowell, Robert. "Thomas, Bishop and Williams," *The Sewanee Review,* LV (Summer 1947), 493-504.

———. *"Paterson* II," *The Nation,* CLXVI (June 19, 1948), 692-694.

———. "William Carlos Williams," *Hudson Review,* XIV (Winter 1961-62), 530-536.

Martz, Louis. "Recent Poetry," *The Yale Review,* XXXVIII (Autumn 1948), 144-151.

———. "The Unicorn in *Paterson:* William Carlos Williams," *Thought,* XXXV (Winter 1960), 537-554.

Massie, Lillian. "Narrative and Symbol in *Paterson*," unpublished dissertation, University of Arkansas, 1955.

Matthiessen, F. O. *The Responsibilities of the Critic*. New York: Oxford University Press, 1952.

Miles, Josephine. *The Primary Language of Poetry in the 1940's*. Berkeley: University of California Press, 1951.

Moore, Marianne. "A Poet of the Quattrocento," *The Dial*, LXXXII (March 1927), 213-215.

———. "Things Others Never Notice," *Poetry*, XLIV (May 1934), 103-106.

Morgan, Frederick. "William Carlos Williams: Imagery, Rhythm, and Form," *The Sewanee Review*, LV (October-December 1947), 675-691.

Munson, Gorham B. *Destinations: A Canvass of American Literature since 1900*. New York: J. H. Sears and Co., Inc., 1928.

Nash, Ralph. "The Use of Prose in *Paterson*," *Perspective*, VI, No. 4 (Autumn 1953), 191-199.

O'Connor, William Van. "Sentient America—Gross, Directionless," *Saturday Review*, XXXI (September 25, 1948), 30.

Olson, Charles. *Projective Verse*. Brooklyn: Totem Press, 1959.

Ostrom, Alan B. "The Poetic World of William Carlos Williams," unpublished dissertation, Columbia University, 1959.

Pearce, Roy Harvey. *The Continuity of American Poetry*. Princeton: Princeton University Press, 1961.

———. "The Poet as Person," *The Yale Review*, XLI (March 1952), 421-440.

Pearson, Norman Holmes. "Williams, New Jersey," *The Literary Review*, I (Autumn 1957), 29-36. (Issue devoted to many articles and items concerning Dr. Williams.)

Pound, Ezra. "Dr. Williams' Position," *The Dial*, LXXXV (November 1928), 395-404.

———. "A Few Don'ts by an Imagiste," *Poetry*, I (1913), 200-206.

Quevado, Francisco de. *The Dog and the Fever*, trans. William Carlos Williams and Raquel Heléne Williams. Hamden, Conn.: The Shoe String Press, 1954.

Quinn, Sister M. Bernetta. *The Metamorphic Tradition in Modern Poetry*. New Brunswick, New Jersey: Rutgers University Press, 1955.

Rakosi, Carl. "William Carlos Williams," *The Symposium* (October 1933), 332-334.

Rexroth, Kenneth. "The Influence of French Poetry on American" and "A Public Letter for William Carlos Williams' Seventy-fifth

Birthday" in *Assays*. Norfolk, Conn.: New Directions, 1961, pp. 143-174 and 202-205.

―――. "A Poet Sums Up," *New York Times Books* (March 28, 1954), p. 5.

Riding, Laura and Robert Graves. *A Survey of Modernist Poetry*. London: William Heinemann, Ltd., 1929.

Rosenfeld, Isaac. "The Poetry and Wisdom of *Paterson*," *The Nation*, CLXIII (August 24, 1946), 216-217.

Rosenfeld, Paul. *Port of New York*. New York: Harcourt, Brace and Co., 1924.

Rosenthal, M. L. *The Modern Poets: A Critical Introduction*. New York: Oxford University Press, 1960.

―――. "Salvo for William Carlos Williams," *The Nation*, CLXXX-VI (May 31, 1958), 497.

Salomon, I. L. "Candor and Science," *Saturday Review*, XXXV (March 15, 1952), 14.

Shapiro, Karl. *In Defense of Ignorance*. New York: Random House, 1952.

Siegel, Eli. "T. S. Eliot and William Carlos Williams: A Distinction," *University of Kansas City Review*, XXII (October 1955), 41-43.

Slate, Joseph Evans. "William Carlos Williams' Image of America," unpublished dissertation, University of Wisconsin, 1957.

Solt, Mary Ellen. "William Carlos Williams: Idiom and Structure," *The Massachusetts Review*, III, No. 2 (Winter 1962), 304-318.

―――. "William Carlos Williams: Poems in the American Idiom," *Folio*, XXV, No. 1 (1960), 3-28.

Soupault, Phillippe. *Last Nights of Paris*, trans. William Carlos Williams. New York: The Macaulay Co., 1929.

Southworth, James G. *More Modern American Poets*. New York: The Macmillan Co., 1954.

Spears, Monroe K. "The Failure of Language," *Poetry*, LXXVI (April 1950), 39-44.

Stearns, Marshall W. "Syntax, Sense and Sound in Dr. Williams," *Poetry*, LXVI (April 1945), 35-40.

Stephens, Alan. "Dr. Williams and Tradition," *Poetry*, CI, No. 5 (February 1963), 360-362.

Sutton, Walter. "Dr. Williams' *Paterson* and the Quest for Form," *Criticism*, II (Summer 1960), 242-259.

―――. "A Visit with William Carlos Williams," *Minnesota Review*, I (1961), 309-324.

Sweeney, John L. "Review of *The Broken Span*," *The Yale Review*, XXX (Summer 1941), 819.

Taupin, René. *L'Influence du Symbolisme Français sur La Poésie Américaine*. Paris: H. Champion, 1929.

Theocritus. *The Idylls of Theocritus in English Verse,* trans. W. Douglas P. Hill. Eton, England: Shakespeare Head Press, 1959.

Thirlwall, John C. "The Lost Poems of William Carlos Williams" or "The Past Recaptured," *New Directions 16* (1957), 3-45.

———. "Ten Years of a New Rhythm," Closing note to *Pictures from Brueghel.* Norfolk, Conn.: New Directions, 1962. Pages 183-184.

———. "Two Cities: Paris and Paterson," *The Massachusetts Review,* III, No. 2 (Winter 1962), 284-291.

———. "William Carlos Williams as Correspondent," *The Literary Review,* I, No. 1 (Autumn 1957), 13-28.

———. "William Carlos Williams' *Paterson:* The Search for the Redeeming Language—A Personal Epic in Five Parts," *New Directions 17* (1961), 252-310.

Turnbull, Gael. "A Visit to WCW: September, 1958," *The Massachusetts Review,* III, No. 2 (Winter 1962), 297-300.

Tyler, Parker. "The Poet of *Paterson* Book One," *Briarcliff Quarterly,* III (October 1946), 168-175. (Issue devoted to Williams materials.)

Untermeyer, Louis. "Experiment and Tradition," *The Yale Review,* XXVIII (Spring 1939), 612.

Wheelwright, Phillip. "Poetry, Myth, and Reality," *The Language of Poetry,* ed. Allen Tate. Princeton: Princeton University Press, 1942. Pages 3-33.

Wilbur, Richard. "7 Poets," *The Sewanee Review,* LVIII (January 1950), 130-143.

Willingham, John R. "Partisan of the Arts," *The Nation,* CLXXX (January 22, 1955), 78.

Wilson, Edmund. *The Triple Thinkers.* New York: Harcourt, Brace and Company, 1948.

Wilson, T. C. "The Example of Dr. Williams," *Poetry,* LXVIII (May 1946), 105-107.

Winters, Yvor. *In Defense of Reason.* New York: The Swallow Press and William Morrow and Co., 1947.

———. "Poetry of Feeling," *The Kenyon Review,* I, No. 1 (January 1939), 104-107.

Zabriskie, George. "The Geography of *Paterson,*" *Perspective,* VI, No. 4 (Autumn 1953), 201-216.

Zukofsky, Louis. "American Poetry 1920-30," *The Symposium* (January 1931), 60-84.

———. " 'The Best Human Value,' " *The Nation,* CLXXXVI (May 31, 1958), 500-502.

———. "An Old Note on William Carlos Williams," *The Massachusetts Review,* III, No. 2 (Winter 1962), 301-302.

Index

Abstractions, 46ff., 66, 70, 124, 125
Allusion, 14
Ambiguity, 120
America, 8
American idiom, 7–9, 36–37, 46ff., 62–63, 75, 110ff.
Aristotle, 10
Arnold, Matthew, 21
Art, 20, 29ff., 69, 102, 108, 115–116, 117, 127, 133–134; *see also* Painting
Auditory quality, 85; *see also* Music

Botticelli, Sandro, 21
Bridge, The, 99
Brueghel, Pieter, 21, 73–74, 130

Caesura, 86, 87
Cantos, The, 99
Cézanne, Paul, 21, 130
Change, 18, 29, 62
Char, René, 33, 61
Chronological organization, 64, 99–100, 114
Ciardi, John, 6
Complex view, 63, 67–68, 73, 124n.
Composition-by-field, 16
Concentration, 11–12, 44, 48, 60–62, 83, 118ff., 125, 126
Concepts, religious, *see* Religious concepts
Convergence, 101
Conversation, 44, 121
Cook, Albert, 100
Counterpoint, 109–110